Get a Lift!

Devotions for Church Leaders

Jeanette Groth

CPH™
SAINT LOUIS

To my husband, Charles A. Groth,
for the constant love and support
that undergirds all my endeavors and
To my international friends with the prayer that
God will use me as a witness to them.

Copyright ©1994 Concordia Publishing House
3558 S. Jefferson Avenue, St. Louis, MO 63118-3968
Manufactured in the United States of America

Library of Congress Cataloging-in-Publication Data

Groth, Jeanette L., 1947–
    Get a lift! : devotions for church leaders / Jeanette L. Groth.
        p.2p   cm.
        ISBN 0-570-04634-3
        1. Devotional exercises. I. Title.
    BV4832.2.G695   1994
    242' .69—dc20   93-30288

1 2 3 4 5 6 7 8 9 10   03 02 01 99 98 97 96 95 94

Contents

⛫

Chosen

But you are a chosen people, a royal priesthood, a holy nation, a people belonging to God, that you may declare the praises of Him who called you out of darkness into His wonderful light. Once you were not a people, but now you are the people of God; once you had not received mercy, but now you have received mercy. 1 Peter 2:9–10

So much of life is spent trying to be a somebody. People use countless means to develop their identity. Some wear distinctive clothing. Others are known by the car they drive. Attention for others comes from efficiency in a job. Today's Bible section reminds us that at one time we were all "nobodies." We were not a people. We lived in darkness. We had not received mercy.

But then the change! We were called out of this darkness—including lack of distinction—by Christ. *Chosen!* What a powerful word. Do you remember it? The time you were picked first for the game. The time you were selected for a special honor or club. Being chosen, in itself, gives one a marvelous feeling of worth. But our feelings go much deeper. We are not just chosen, but chosen by Christ. The Savior, our Lord, has picked us. He has called us to be His own.

He has given us the wonderful gifts of forgiveness, hope, and eternal life. Our Savior has shown us mercy and brought us into the uplifting, empowering path of His light.

Stand up straight. Be filled with the wonderful message of your true identity. You are a chosen person. You are part of a royal priesthood. You belong to God. Breathe in the uniqueness and power that He alone brings you through Word and Sacrament.

Now you're ready for service in the classroom, the congregation, the world. You can declare His praises confidently, for He has made you what you are. He has set you apart for His service. He has given you purpose and value. Shout it out! You're a somebody when chosen by Him.

Prayer

Sometimes, Lord, I feel so worthless. I can't think of anything that makes me valued or special. Remind me that YOU called me to be YOUR own. YOU chose me. Give me boldness to share that empowerment with others as I declare the worth you have given me as my King and my Savior. Amen.

Activity

Find an old picture of yourself. Draw a crown on your head. Put it on your desk or kitchen table to remind you of your value as one chosen by our King.

✠

Redeemed

For you know that it was not with perishable things such as silver or gold that you were redeemed from the empty way of life handed down to you from your forefathers, but with the precious blood of Christ, a lamb without blemish or defect. He was chosen before the creation of the world, but was revealed in these last times for your sake. Through Him you believe in God, who raised Him from the dead and glorified Him, and so your faith and hope are in God. 1 Peter 1:18–21

It is difficult to put a price on objects of great senti-mental value. What is the price tag on the family photo album? What dollar amount goes on the inherited ring? Who can attach monetary worth to a favorite family recipe? If it is hard to place worth on such things, it is even more difficult to place a ransom amount on a loved person. History has recorded astro-nomical amounts paid to release ransom victims from their captors.

The greatest ransom amount ever paid has *your* name attached to it. The ransom paid was not gold or silver. That would be far too impersonal and far too slight. The ransom paid for you was the life of God's Son. God's Son died for YOU! "He was chosen before the creation of the world, but was revealed in these last times for your sake."

It is not who you are. It is not your great proficiencies or abilities that give you value and worth. You have been ransomed totally out of love. Your Savior, Jesus Christ, loved you so much that He gave His life for you to free you from the bondage of sin and bring you forgiveness, power for living, and life eternal.

You have been bought with a great price. You have been redeemed for a purpose. Share with others the value and worth that come from the great redemption Christ has won for them.

Prayer
Thank You, Father, for thinking enough of me to sacrifice the life of Your Son. Forgive me for the times I forget my worth in Your eyes. Empower me to share the good news of my redemption with all I meet today. Amen.

Activity
Write a note to homebound or hospitalized individuals in your congregation to remind them of their worth. Tell them of the great ransom price that has been paid for them—the life of Jesus their Savior.

⁜

Gifted

It was He who gave some to be apostles, some to be prophets, some to be evangelists, and some to be pastors and teachers, to prepare God's people for works of service, so that the body of Christ may be built up until we all reach unity in the faith and in the knowledge of the Son of God and become mature, attaining to the whole measure of the fullness of Christ. Ephesians 4:11–13

Much has been written today about education. We recognize the marvelous abilities that God has bestowed upon people who are able to learn and excel in many areas of academia. We read of early readers, young computer whizzes, and adolescent college graduates.

The term *gifted* itself causes us to do some thinking. Giftedness is nothing of a person's own doing. The gift is undeserved—a blessing from God to be developed in His service.

Each Christian worker might wear a tag reading *Gifted*. Today's Bible section reminds us of the many gifts that God gives to His church. Some are prophets, evangelists, pastors, teachers . . . and we could add countless more titles if we were to comprise a complete list from the whole of Scripture. We would find that God has gifted His servants with many talents and abilities to help the world "[know] the Son of God and become mature, attaining to the whole measure of the fullness of Christ."

These talents and abilities are not of our own doing. There is no merit or worthiness in ourselves that causes God to bestow these gifts on us. Quite the contrary. We deserve none of these marvelous blessings.

As with all gifts, the thanks and praise belong to the giver. When we see God's kingdom grow, our praise goes to the giver, our heavenly Father. It is He who provides all that is needed in the church to truly accomplish His purposes. It is He who uses mere humans to share the marvelous news that Jesus has suffered, died, and rose for all mankind. What gifts! What a Giver!

Prayer

Dear Giver of all Gifts, thank You that You have gifted me for service in Your kingdom. Help me to remember that the gifts You give to the church accomplish the things that You will. Remind me that You give me worth and strength to share Your message in the way that is most fitting. Amen.

Activity

Write a letter to someone who, as a gift to the church, has helped you grow in faith and commitment to Christ.

✠

Unafraid

Ignoring what they said, Jesus told the syna-gogue ruler, "Don't be afraid; just believe." Mark 5:36

Make a list of the things you fear. Imagine the worst that could happen if the things you fear came to be.

Jairus was filled with fear. His daughter was ill and he had come to Jesus to beg for healing. As Jesus accompanied him to his home, the word came. His child was dead. No need to bother the Master anymore. His worst fears had been realized. His child would no longer greet him with a happy smile or delight him with her play.

Jesus knew the fear that gripped the synagogue ruler's heart. "Don't be afraid; just believe." He said, Jesus words seemed to mock reality. Why shouldn't Jairus fear? Death had claimed his child. His worst fear had been realized.

But Jesus continued with the fearful man to his home. There He put aside the wailing crowds and announced that the child was not dead, but sleeping. Jairus' faith became sight as Jesus called the little girl to rise.

Jesus calms our worst fears. He alone can turn the worst things that happen to us into the best as we trust the Father's promise to work all things out for our ulti-

11

mate, eternal good. God is in control. Christ takes away our greatest fear—the fear of death—with the power of His resurrection. He gives the peace of sins forgiven and the power of His Spirit to walk beside us. "Don't be afraid, only believe."

Prayer

Father, help me believe that You can turn my worst fears into good. Strengthen my belief in Your Son, my Savior, who removes the great fear of death. Hold me in Your hands that I may feel Your peace and security. Amen.

Activity

Change your fear list into your prayer list.

✠

Willing

"Watch and pray so that you will not fall into temptation. The spirit is willing, but the body is weak." Mark 14:38

The coach huddled his players and eyed his young recruits. Their eagerness was evident; their dedication superb. But temptations surrounded them, threatening to draw them away from the task at hand into worldly pleasures. They had to train, concentrate, and make a total commitment to be victorious.

Our Savior huddled His disciples around Him. They trained with Him. Their willingness was evident. But all around the world called them to be concerned about physical needs and pleasures. Jesus called them to total commitment of spirit and body.

God seeks the same from each of His committed workers today. Motivated by the great love He showed us in the gift of His Son, we long to serve Him. But our humanity gets in the way. We need one more hour of sleep. Physical needs crowd out spiritual ones. Things that need to be done at home and relaxing pleasures call us away from one more task at church. The spirit is willing, but our humanity makes us weak.

How wonderful that our Savior understands our humanity! He too was human and experienced the temptations that surround us every day. He knows how the world reaches out to pull us into its clutches, away from the total commitment of a life of Christian service.

Yes, Jesus understands our temptations, but He did not give into them. He carried the burden of our lack of commitment to the cross. Once, for all, He died to pay the price of our sins and rose to win us a new life of service with Him.

Our great Coach meets us in His Word, not just to strengthen our willingness, but to also strengthen our body. God's Spirit lives within us and makes our bodies His temple. His power helps us overcome the temptations that lure our body away from the actions our willingness demands. Word and Sacrament empower us to serve God with total commitment. We rise above the call of our human nature with the power of His Spirit.

Prayer
Dear Jesus, Help me to be totally committed in service to you. Strengthen my willingness to serve You and keep selfish needs from getting in the way of the work You call me to do. Amen.

Activity
Do some exercises to strengthen your body. How does a fit body play into Christian commitment?

⊹

Enabled

He has raised up a horn of salvation for us in the house of His servant David (as He said through His holy prophets of long ago), salvation from our enemies and from the hand of all who hate us—to show mercy to our fathers and to remember His holy covenant, the oath He swore to our father Abraham: to rescue us from the hand of our enemies, and to enable us to serve Him without fear in holiness and righteousness before Him all our days. Luke 1:69–75

We use the term *disabled* to define a segment of our population who deal with some type of impairment. Proper training and support prevent disabilities from becoming handicaps. Those who do not know Jesus as their Lord and Savior suffer a disability that is indeed a handicap. They are crippled by sin. They have no hope of eternal life.

As Christians, we wear the label "enabled." By grace, through the power of the Holy Spirit, Christians know their Lord and Savior. Their sins are forgiven. They live a new life, confident in the hope of life eternal and a home in heaven.

The Christian is also enabled to serve boldly, without fear. God's indwelling Holy Spirit gives us the words to speak which accomplish His purpose and plan. We carry the good news of salvation to persons disabled by sin.

The world may marvel at the boldness of enabled Christians. In the power of God's Spirit we withstand discomfort, hardship, and persecution. We meet distant tribes or scoffers in the church meeting room, proudly proclaiming His Gospel.

What is your job today? Does it seem too difficult? Do you feel discouraged? Do obstacles seem disabling? You have been rescued. God enables you to serve with power and confidence.

Prayer
Dear Jesus, You empower me for service. Let this enabling banish my fear and be my strength. Amen.

Activity
Place a note where you will see it today. Let it simply say, "Enabled." When facing fears or doubts, remember Christ's enabling power.

✠

Unashamed

However, if you suffer as a Christian, do not be ashamed, but praise God that you bear that name. 1 Peter 4:16

Have you ever been tempted to hide your Christian vocation? Sometimes other professions and community commitments seem so much more glamorous than spending time at church. The world assigns little value to church work. Hollywood and the media often portray the Christian worker as inept, blundering, and foolish. We may feel tempted to hide our commitment for Christ to avoid the charitable comments or snickers.

But our God encourages us not to be ashamed. He who has emboldened, empowered, and equipped us for His service wants us to proudly bear the name of Christian. Our pride does not stem from anything that we have accomplished. We are sinners. We have missed the mark.

Our pride and distinction comes from who we serve. Just as the courtiers in times of old were proud to be associated with their king, we are proud to be connected to our Savior and King, Jesus Christ. We celebrate the victory He has accomplished. Our Savior has conquered sin, death, and the devil. Best of all,

His victory is our victory. Because He lives, we, too, can live.

Pay attention the next time you watch a sports team celebrate victory. There is no shame in being associated with a winner. A victorious team shouts with joy. We find that joy in Christian service. We are more than conquerors because of Christ's victory. We are privileged to share the victory message. The message we share brings life and salvation to all who believe it. When earthly kingdoms crumble, when worldly goods decay, the message that we bring will endure and continue as a mighty power. Be proud of the Savior you serve. There is no shame in service of this King.

Prayer
Lord, make me proud to be a servant of Jesus Christ. Help me to boldly serve You today. Amen.

Activity
Share with one person a joy you have experienced in your life as a servant of Jesus Christ.

✠

Strengthened

"My grace is sufficient for you, for My power is made perfect in weakness." Therefore I will boast all the more gladly about my weaknesses, so that Christ's power may rest on me. That is why, for Christ's sake, I delight in weaknesses, in insults, in hardships, in persecutions, in difficulties. For when I am weak, then I am strong.
2 Corinthians 12:9–10

Everyone has known the frustration of wanting to step in and make a task easier for someone you love. Perhaps you have watched a child do a difficult task that would be relatively effortless for you. Still the child insists, "I can do it myself." You may have experienced the inner struggle that comes when you watch a physically challenged friend struggle and insist that no help is needed. You know the person can accomplish the task, yet out of love you really want to give assistance.

Each day our God watches us struggle in our weaknesses. As we try to go it on our own, He must long to say, "If only you would let Me take your weakness and support you with My strength."

There is no great achievement in going it alone when someone is there to support you. A wise person knows that using resources wisely is the key to success. The wise Christian worker assesses his resources. What is it that gets the job done? What makes work and witness most effective?

In the Bible reading, Paul calls for us to empty ourselves of all pretense. It is not we who are strong, but Christ who lives within us. His atoning sacrifice paid the price for all our sins and won for us God's forgiveness. We can endure all that the world offers when we realize that Christ's power is made perfect in our human weakness. With Paul we boldly face difficulties and hardships, knowing Christ's strength wins our victory.

Prayer
Dear Lord, remind me that my strength comes from You. Turn my self-will into Your will. Amen.

Activity
Acknowledge God's strength in your life to someone today.

Spoken For

My dear children, I write this to you so that you will not sin. But if anybody does sin, we have One who speaks to the Father in our defense— Jesus Christ, the Righteous One. He is the atoning sacrifice for our sins, and not only for ours but also for the sins of the whole world. 1 John 2:1–2

It is always good to have someone put in a good word for you. It may be someone attesting to your qualifications as you apply for a new job. It might be a character witness in a court of law. It may be a friend speaking to an interested date. We all feel good about people who speak about us in positive ways.

Our Lord Jesus Christ always speaks for us. He stands at the right hand of God the Father, ready to speak on our behalf when we sin. Perhaps He reminds the Father that these dastardly sins are the very ones for which He suffered and died. They have been covered with the robe of righteousness that He has won for us.

When we try to obey all of God's commands, we fall far short of perfection. Sins of omission and commission fill our everyday lives. These, too, are the sins that nailed our Savior to the tree. Thankfully, Christ stands ready as our defense.

All Christians throughout the world have this wonderful advocate. Jesus speaks for each and every Christian, announcing the salvation and forgiveness that belong to them.

It's wonderful to have reliable friends speak up for us. Their witness brings credibility to our endeavors and lifts our spirits. It's more wonderful to have our Savior, Jesus Christ speak up for us. His witness brings salvation and eternal life.

Prayer
Lord, I know that I have sinned. What a comfort that You are there at the throne of the heavenly Father pleading for me. It is good to know that when the Father looks at me, He does not see my sins, but the redemption that You have won for me. Amen.

Activity
Speak a good word for someone who could use your support.

Inhabited

*I have been crucified with Christ and I no
longer live, but Christ lives in me. The life I live
in the body, I live by faith in the Son of God, who
loved me and gave Himself for me. Galatians 2:20*

An interesting part of any trip to Hollywood is a tour
through spectacular residential areas. A good tour
guide shares the real estate value of the homes passed.
The prices command gasps of amazement. As the tour
progresses, the guide points out the homes of movie
stars, and the list price soars. Tourists realize that it is
not the real estate that commands the value, but the
star who lives inside the home.

The same is the case for every redeemed child of
God. The worth that is announced is not the value of
the person. It has nothing to do with talents and abili-
ties, a beautiful exterior, or a great body and good hair.
Nor is it the ability to do the job that gives a child of
God worth.

True worth comes from the One who lives inside
us. St. Paul states it clearly—"Christ lives in me." It is
the atoning work of Christ, then, which gives us value.
His indwelling is our claim to fame and distinction.

All of us at times look in the mirror or probe our
inner selves to try and find qualities that make us feel
worthwhile. This self-probing can only leave us lack-

ing esteem. In moments of depression and despair, we feel that we are worthless. Others attack the job we have done, or the project we have planned, and our worth collapses around us. It is then that we need to reread today's Bible verse and remember that our worth comes from our Lord and Savior, Jesus Christ.

Jesus, our indwelling Lord, loves us and gave Himself for us. His is not the superficial here-today-and-gone-tomorrow kind of love. It is a love that stays, makes a home within us, and continues to grow. It is love that knows no measure, love that has gone all the way for us—all the way to the cross of Calvary, the depths of hell, and the heights of resurrection victory.

When words such as "worthless," "empty," and "alone" come to mind, remember the indwelling Christ who loves you, lives within you, and gives all of your life meaning and value. Rejoice in the chance to share His love with others so that they, too, can become valued children of God.

Prayer
Dear Jesus, thank You for living in me. Remind me always that with You I have perpetual value and worth. Amen.

Activity
Post a real estate ad in you line of vision. Let it remind you of who lives in you, and the many who have vacant space in their lives.

✠

Time Off

The LORD said, "Go out and stand on the mountain in the presence of the LORD, for the LORD is about to pass by." Then a great and powerful wind tore the mountains apart and shattered the rocks before the LORD, but the LORD was not in the wind. After the wind there was an earthquake, but the LORD was not in the earthquake. After the earthquake came a fire, but the LORD was not in the fire. And after the fire came a gentle whisper. When Elijah heard it, he pulled his cloak over his face and went out and stood at the mouth of the cave. Then a voice said to him, "What are you doing here, Elijah?" 1 Kings 19:11–13

Elijah had been busy doing the work of the Lord. No one seemed to appreciate how great the job was. The Israelites had rejected the Lord. They had broken down the altars of the true God. They were seeking Elijah and trying to kill him.

Can you identify with this picture? Does it seem to you at times that you are the only one left working for the Lord? The pressures of the job. The demands of students, counselees, meetings, and services seem to press after you. Sometimes you, too, may feel like saying,"I am the only one left, and now they are trying to kill me too."

Then go out and stand on the "mountain"—wherever it is for you. Perhaps it is a peaceful fishing hole or a favorite movie theater. In that moment apart let God come to you to refresh you. For in that place, in that moment, God can renew you and you may hear Him ask, "What are you doing here . . . ?"

As you meet your God in a place set apart, you can reevaluate and reassess the job that is before you. Maybe in these moments of relaxation you can refocus and reestablish the priorities that are before you. Just what will God have you do? Feel the renewal of the strength He brings you in His gentle whisper.

So run away and renew. Listen to God's voice—His holy Word. It is there you will hear the Good News of your forgiveness and renewal through the life, death, and resurrection of His Son. Then go back the way you came. Regroup your forces and serve the Lord.

Prayer
Dear Lord, I need to hear Your gentle whisper. I need Your prodding and patience to get me going again. Help me to be renewed by Your Spirit so that I may serve You with gladness all the days of my life. Amen.

Activity
Relax and do something just for the fun of it.

☩

Renewal

*He gives strength to the weary and increases
the power of the weak. Even youths grow tired
and weary, and young men stumble and fall; but
those who hope in the LORD will renew their
strength. They will soar on wings like eagles; they
will run and not grow weary, they will walk and
not be faint. Isaiah 40:29–31*

Many exercises and techniques can revitalize the
weary. Some say deep breathing gives the weary a lift.
When driving, an open window may provide needed
stimulation. Some say a caffeinated beverage gives
them the lift they need to keep going in moments of
drowsiness.

God has a wonderful formula for strength
renewal. He encourages His followers to hope in the
Lord. This hope is not a wishful kind of thinking. It is
not the I-hope-we'll-have-Jell-O-for-supper kind of
hope, when we know there isn't a box of Jell-O in the
house. The hope that our God encourages in us is the
sure and certain hope that belongs only to those who
know Jesus as their Lord and Savior. This hope is
founded in the message that Jesus died and rose to
save those who believe in Him. This hope is the message of victory that comes from knowing that our Savior has conquered the might of the devil and risen vic-

torious. This victory brings Christians the sure hope that they, too, are victorious.

In the weary moments of life, in the valleys of sadness when life seems to drag on and tire out even the bravest Christian soldiers, this sure hope brings strength and renewal. This sure hope and certain future helps weary Christians soar. This hope helps tired Christians run and not grow tired. They know where the race leads. It enables them to walk the way that God has planned, and not be faint.

If you are weary today, remember the sure hope God gives you. Christ's victory is tabulated to your account. Know where your road leads as you bring the message of life and salvation to those around you. Christ's everlasting arms are underneath you to support you and around you to protect you. Now soar.

Prayer
Dear Lord, when I feel weary renew me and remind me of the sure hope that You give me. Let me be uplifted by the victory that is mine through Your victory over sin and death. Amen.

Activity
Breathe deeply. With each deep breath say a Bible verse that reminds you of your strength in Jesus.

Upheld

So do not fear, for I am with you; do not be dismayed, for I am your God. I will strengthen you and help you; I will uphold you with My righteous right hand. Isaiah 41:10

The plant is top-heavy with tomatoes. Without the stake the tomatoes would lie on the ground, rot, and be wasted. It is the stake that gives the tomato plant strength and enables it to bear fruit. The stake is the plant's support.

The battle is fierce. Israel wins, but only when Moses' hands are raised. And so Aaron supports Moses' hands. He holds them up until the victory is won.

Do you feel them—the hands that are holding you? When your battle is fierce and long, they are there. They are your support. Without God's support you would be dragged down, afraid, and fruitless. Without those hands so much of what you do would be rotten and wasted.

You can be productive. Our God reminds you that you need not be afraid. He has selected you for your job. He has called you to be His own through Baptism and His Word. He has pulled you into Christian service with the powerful magnet of His living Word.

God's hands are beneath you. The hands that felt the pierce of nails when Christ carried your sins to the cross, that brought you light and life eternal, are there daily to bring you support and love. Rely on those supporting hands when the world around you tries to defeat you and draw you away from the mission you have been called to pursue.

God's hands are there to support you when others let you down. When you feel the world's troubles pulling you down, fall back into the supporting arms of your heavenly Father. When your strength fails, know that His is there. When you are frail, His strong arms bring you the power to carry on. You are never alone.

Prayer
At times, dear Father, I feel that I am being dragged down by the evil around me. I feel that I am helpless and alone. Let me know that You will help me to accomplish the tasks You have in mind, and will support me with your strong hands. Amen.

Activity
Write a letter of support to a fellow Christian who may need you as "arm support" today.

✠

I Can Do It

*I can do everything through Him who gives
me strength. Philippians 4:13*

How many times have you said it? "I can't do it. I can't
do one more thing." Perhaps you felt you were at your
breaking point. Physically and mentally you were han-
dling all that you could. Then a committee or a person
asked for more—more time, more commitment, more
energy. Perhaps as you read this, you are feeling overwhelmed with what you have to do and with the lack
of time you have to do it in.

God's Word offers hope. The Word of God you
just read reminds you of a power that is there for the
asking. It is the wonderful power of God that reminds
us that we are right. *We* cannot do it. It is Christ who
lives in us who enables us and gives us the strength,
energy, and mind-set to go ahead and tackle the seem-
ingly insurmountable tasks that stand before us. Paul
clearly remembers the source of his strength. It is
through Christ that we can accomplish all things.

That doesn't mean that we can go into overload
or blame God when we take on too much and then
cannot accomplish everything. The things that we can
accomplish are the things that are in line with His will
and plan. He has blessed us with the ability to plan and
organize the time that He has given us.

What tasks seem impossible? Take it to your time management specialist, Jesus Christ. He can help you to use the time that He gives you wisely for His plan and purpose. Remember that the Spirit lives within you. He fills your lack with His power and wisdom. Think of your Savior. He took time aside, time to pray, time to rejuvenate in communion with His Father. Remember the Garden of Gethsemane. The Father sent angels to strengthen Christ for the great task of salvation set before Him.

You can do it! You can do all things with His power. You are redeemed, restored, forgiven. God's power is yours as you face the task before you.

Prayer
Dear heavenly Father, strengthen me for service as You did Your own dear Son. Remind me that I can do all the things that You have planned for me to do with the strength that You give me. Amen.

Activity
Write today's Bible verse in your planning calendar.

✠

Christ in Me

*I have been crucified with Christ and I no
longer live, but Christ lives in me. The life I live
in the body, I live by faith in the Son of God, who
loved me and gave Himself for me. Galatians 2:20*

"I just don't have it in me." "It's what's inside that
counts." We often speak of strength and feelings as
dwelling within a person. When we say we don't have it
in us, we mean to say that there is no way we can bring
ourselves to face or accomplish the task at hand. When
we speak about that which is inside being valuable, we
are often referring to good thoughts, benevolent qualities, or beautiful attitudes.

St. Paul also talks about what is inside as being the
power, strength, and beauty for daily living. For the
Christian what is inside is Christ. Christ dwells within
the Christian through Word and Sacrament. When
doubts and depression cripple, the indwelling Christ
casts aside fear with the reminder that He died, rose,
and won the victory over sin, death, and the devil. The
knowledge that Christ lives within us gives faith and
purpose to life. The Christian is dead. He is dead to
sin. But because Christ lives within him he is alive to
witness and service. He is alive to the marvelous news
that heaven is his home.

Picture a colorful piñata. It is merely a decoration. When it is broken open, the candy inside brings joy to the children who surround it. We bring joy when we proclaim the indwelling Christ to those who surround us.

Strength for today, then, comes from within. Meaning and direction come from within. Not because of some vague personal power, or psychological phenomenon, but because within us is the Christ who loved us enough to give His life.

Prayer
Dear God, when I need strength and purpose for living, help me to look within to my constant companion—the indwelling Christ. Let Him give my life direction and strength in difficult times. Amen.

Activity
Write a note to your indwelling Christ thanking Him for His daily presence in your life.

✠

No One against Us

What, then, shall we say in response to this?
If God is for us, who can be against us? He who
did not spare His own Son, but gave Him up for
us all—how will He not also, along with Him,
graciously give us all things? Romans 8:31–32

Sometimes we do not know how to answer those who cause us trouble or who speak against us. We are upset when others find fault and criticize our ideas. We are troubled when others seek ways to undermine our plans and work against decisions and actions we have taken. At times it seems that we stand alone with everyone and everything against us.

There is One, our Lord and Savior Jesus Christ, who is always on our side. That does not mean that He takes our side in every problem or quarrel. It does mean that in the issue of Satan vs. Us He is our support and defense. When others chip away at the foundation of our faith, Jesus Christ speaks up in His Word and precious supper to remind us that He died so that we can claim forgiveness, salvation, eternal life.

Our God gives us all that we need for life. Jesus came to bring us life, life in all its fullness. He faced angry criticism from church leaders—to the point of giving His own life. That sacrifice is the event that motivates us to keep at our tasks, even in the face of criticism.

When others are against you, remember who stands by your side at the heavenly throne. Remember your advocate, Jesus Christ, the Righteous One. He is there with His legions of power to protect, to defend, and finally to lead you to your eternal home.

Prayer
Dear Jesus, sometimes it seems that everyone is against me. It helps to know that in matters of salvation, You are always there to plead my case. Amen.

Activity
Pray for those who seem to always be against Your plans and ideas.

✠

Something Lasting

*"All men are like grass, and all their glory is
like the flowers of the field; the grass withers and
the flowers fall, but the word of the Lord stands
forever." 1 Peter 1:24–25*

So many things in life are temporary. We look at buildings one day only to see them destroyed by the wrecking ball the next. We see a house clean and ready for guests and then the day after their arrival, we note its disarray. We read news stories and magazine articles about famous entertainers and watch their fame turn to ignominity. "Here today, gone tomorrow" seems to be the philosophy that rules our world.

How wonderful it is for us, then, to have a job that really lasts! Those of us who share God's Word, the Holy Scriptures, share the essence of something that lasts forever. God's Word stands the test of time. God's Word carries a message for all ages. God's Word brings eternal dimension to the lives it touches.

While others build with temporary materials, those of us who build with God's Word create an enduring medium. When God's Word changes hearts and lives, they are changed for eternity. Kings have tried to silence this Word. Presidents have thwarted it. People have attempted to hide, chain, or manipulate it. But God's Word endures. The news that Christ fulfilled the Law in our stead and sacrificed His life for ours stands for all time.

What a job! We have a task—no matter what our daily occupation—with a lasting, eternal dimension. Praise God for the stability of His Word.

Prayer
Dear Savior, sometimes I get discouraged with my occupation and the fragility of much that surrounds me. Remind me, then, of the eternal nature of Your Word. Let me know that while kingdoms rise and fall, the message I have to share lasts eternally. Amen.

Activity
Write the words "the word of the Lord stands forever" on a rock. Place it on your desk or kitchen table as a reminder that your task of sharing God's Word has an eternal dimension.

✠

Worldwide Fellowship

Be self-controlled and alert. Your enemy the devil prowls around like a roaring lion looking for someone to devour. Resist him, standing firm in the faith, because you know that your brothers throughout the world are undergoing the same kind of sufferings. 1 Peter 5:8–9

Do you ever feel all alone? Does it seem to you that you are the only one fighting the battle against the devil? Do you feel a separation from others who live in the world and follow the calls of materialism, popularity, and self-interest?

When this sense of loneliness overwhelms you, think of the wonderful words of today's Bible section. Others, too, endure the devil's prowling. We share a fellowship with those all over the world who count themselves followers of Jesus Christ. Those followers are taunted, ignored, and hunted as we are. Satan seeks to destroy this fellowship and to make each Christian think that he or she stands alone.

But such is not the case. Christians all over the world support each other with prayer and praise. Christians all over the world share the strength that comes from God's Word and Sacrament. We, and Christians all over the world, rejoice in the news that

Christ won our victory over Satan in His atoning work on the cross.

Praise God for the Christian fellowship we share. Pray for Christians undergoing circumstances similar to your own. Be encouraged in the worldwide fellowship that Christ won for you.

Prayer

Lord, I need to be reminded that I am not alone in my fight against the devil's cunning. Help me know that others the world over are fighting, too, to be the witnesses You have called them to be. Give each of us an extra measure of your presence as the devil tries to pull us away. Keep us alert to His treacheries. Protect us. Amen.

Activity

Take a moment to look at a globe. Pick a country and ask God to bless the Christians who witness there. You might write a letter to a missionary in that country telling him of your prayer support.

⊕

Stick with It

See that what you have heard from the beginning remains in you. If it does, you also will remain in the Son and in the Father. And this is what He promised us—even eternal life. 1 John 2:24–25

Persistence pays. Sometimes just sticking with something helps to solve a problem. The persistent problem solver continues to look for solutions. The persistent basketball player works to increase his shots through sheer repetition. The persistent teacher tries countless ways to motivate students and help them find the path to success.

Today's Bible text encourages persistence and tenaciousness. We are to be persistent about clinging to the Word of God. We are to stick with what we have heard about our Lord and Savior, Jesus Christ.

Often times, new ideas, flashy doctrines, outstanding speakers, and contemporary motivational tactics tempt us to try another message than the word that comes from God. In such situations God's Word speaks to you. Be persistent. Stick with what you know. Stick with the age-old Gospel message which, alone, brings forgiveness, life, and salvation.

Prayer

Today it's difficult, Lord, to stick to Your simple Gospel message. So many of the world's messages try to pull me away. I need You to lift me up and give me the power of persistence. Remind me that your Gospel alone can bring me forgiveness, life, and salvation. Amen.

Activity

Find and read a simple child's account of a Bible story. If possible, use a book that you remember from childhood. Let this activity remind you that it is the simple message of what God did for us in the death and resurrection of His Son that leads to eternal life.

⊕

Power to Remain

"Whoever eats My flesh and drinks My blood remains in Me, and I in Him." John 6:56

An infant's attachment to its mother via the umbilical cord is the most intimate and delicate balance in all of nature. Through this miraculous tie, mother and child exchange nutrients and wastes are removed. Without this tie the fetus could not live or grow.

We have such a lifeline. The lifeline connects us with God, through Word and Sacrament. We are intimately tied to our Lord and Savior, Jesus Christ. When we feel weak, it is the nourishment of the Sacrament that gives us strength. The Holy Spirit comes to us in Christ's body and blood and fans our wavering, questioning faith.

How important it is when our faith is lagging, when doubts arise, when we feel depressed and down, that we do not turn away from God's precious meal. He reminds us through this blessed gift that we remain in Him and He remains in us. We are strengthened and rejuvenated by this marvelous meal. God upholds us through His Word and guards us against the devil's attempts to pull us away from our Savior.

Think of it. In the Sacrament we actually take within us the very body of our Lord and Savior, Jesus Christ. The bread *is* His body, broken for us on the cross. The wine *is* His blood, shed for us in redeeming sacrifice. What a comfort to know that He meets our needs and comes within us to sustain us. What a precious balance is this nurturing relationship.

Taste and see that the Lord is good. Let Him bend to your need and erase your doubts and despair with His presence through bread and wine.

Prayer
Lord, let me use the means You have given me of Word and Sacrament to support my frail spirit. Come and remain in me that I may abide in You. Amen.

Activity
Participate in your next opportunity for Holy Communion.

✠

No Orphans

"I will not leave you as orphans; I will come to you." John 14:18

An ad in our Sunday newspaper tugs each week at our heart strings. Children are pictured in a variety of heart-tugging situations. The ad copy describes their problems. Each ad is called "The Waiting Children." The ad closes by explaining how you can end their waiting by adopting these children.

In our verse for today God uses graphic words to remind us that we are not alone. When we feel abandoned, we can be assured that our God will not leave us as orphans. A picture of us could be captioned "The Waiting Children," but we know that our wait will not be in vain. Our Lord and Savior, Jesus Christ, will return to take us to our Father's home. Each day brings us one day closer to that happy reunion.

When the troubles and trials of the world surround us, we can hang on to such promises. Jesus gives us strength as we wait. And we have so much to do. Countless people are orphans, without a relationship with their heavenly Father. They are truly lost and know only the futility and hopelessness of lives filled with guilt, anxiety, and desperation. It is only the Good News that Christ paid the price for their sins, in their stead, on the cross that can bring them hope.

We have a task to do while we wait. Our heavenly Father delights to see us gainfully working to bring others into the family before the day of His Son's return. We will not be orphans. Jesus will come.

Prayer

Dear Jesus, we are waiting for You. Thank You for sending us the Comforter so that we can rely on His enabling power during this waiting time. Bless us as we work while we wait, telling everyone what you have done for us. Amen.

Activity

Visit an older person who is waiting impatiently for Christ's return. Share comfort and pray with that person. Jesus will return. We are not alone.

⊕

Refreshments

Repent, then, and turn to God, so that your sins may be wiped out, that times of refreshing may come from the Lord. Acts 3:19

Refreshments are the high point of many a church meeting. After sitting through a lengthy meeting or serious presentation, enjoying refreshments provides a time of fellowship and sharing. The food is delightful. Perhaps the fellowship is even more refreshing.

All of us need times of refreshment throughout our lives. Sometimes the world crowds in on us. We feel wilted, tired, overwhelmed. How can we continue to function? Where will our strength and motivation come from?

Our Lord knows how to refresh us. His refreshment fills more than just the body. He showers us with the peace and joy of sins forgiven. We are rejuvenated in the knowledge that each day is a new beginning. Our God "remembers our sins no more." "He removes our sins as far as the east is from the west." Past failures, past errors are erased. What a refreshing thought!

Newness brings vitality. A new outfit gives the spirit a lift. A new adventure brings excitement. It is the newness of sins forgiven, life restored, that brings refreshment of the best kind to people who are bogged down with cares, concerns, and rejections. Our God accepts us, loves us, and refreshes us with His forgiveness. It is indeed the basis for new life, new joy, new purpose.

Take a moment for refreshment. Ponder God's gifts of forgiveness, new life, and salvation. Bask in the fellowship that comes from knowing that your Savior loves *you* and gave His life for *you*. Count on God's forgiveness and be boosted by the newness of each day. Look for the power His Spirit brings to daily life to restore, renew, and refresh even the most tired spirit. Taste and see that the Lord is good. What refreshment He alone can bring!

Prayer

Lord, I need the refreshment that You alone can bring. Often I forget that it is You who gives my life purpose and excitement. Buoy me up and refresh me for new service in Your kingdom. Amen.

Activity

Make a simple refreshment for someone whom you know is bogged down with a problem. Be refreshed together as you pray for Christ's presence and guidance.

✠

Let's Stay

"Rabbi, it is good for us to be here. Let us put up three shelters—one for You, one for Moses and one for Elijah." Mark 9:5

"It's time to leave." The words ring out and suddenly the child sets heels down and digs in for a fight. It's hard to leave in the middle of a fun activity. Adults often feel the same way when they must part from family or friends, leave an exciting event, or move on from a particularly interesting vacation spot.

The disciples had just experienced a marvelous sight. They had seen their Savior transfigured before their very eyes. His clothes had become dazzling white. They had seen the patriarchs, Elijah and Moses. How could anything compete with this? The experience had touched their lives and sent their spirits soaring.

And then Peter said it. Let's just stay. Why not? Why leave this mountaintop where they had experienced a tremendous rush of exhilaration and excitement? Could anything be better? Why did life need to go on? Peter wanted that experience and joy to last forever.

Have you ever felt that way? Perhaps the joy of a worship service that is particularly exciting fills your soul. The joy of a child and her wonderful confession of faith might ring in your ears. The excitement of a spiritual convention or meaningful Bible study seems too good to end. Why do we have to go on? Why must we leave the mountaintop?

But today's Bible reading also sees the disciples coming down the mountain. They had work to do. There were more mountains to climb; there were more experiences to encounter and more joys to share.

Our God gives us the joy of mountaintop experiences to equip us for our life of service on the plain. He gives us special joy to put a spring in our step and leads us to new areas of service in His kingdom.

Rejoice in your mountaintop experience. Inhale the Spirit and power that they bring to your life. Then step down and follow the sometimes difficult path of sharing the joy of Jesus, motivating His people, and jarring the world with the message that Christ Jesus came into the world to save sinners.

Prayer

Dear Jesus, the mountaintops are great. Help me to remember them and draw on them as I return to daily service on the plain. Let the boundless joy that comes from Your constant and enabling presence fill my life. Amen.

Activity

Keep a journal of your mountaintop experiences. Read it when the going on the plain gets exceptionally tough.

More Accountable

Not many of you should presume to be teachers, my brothers, because you know that we who teach will be judged more strictly. James 3:1

Have you ever watched children play school? As you watch, you will discover many of their teacher's habits and ways of speaking. The children may talk about subjects dear to that person's heart or mimic the way she corrects a misbehaving student.

Those of us who are professional and volunteer church workers need to recognize the possible pitfalls of our leadership. Others are listening. An error we make could be multiplied many times over. A thoughtless comment could hurt someone without our realizing it. We have a great responsibility to those we teach.

Not only are our words copied, but our actions as well. Just as the child mimics the way the teacher gestures or holds the chalk, those who follow and learn from us may mimic our actions. Actions preach the loudest sermon of all. With the Spirit's aid our patterns of daily living can serve as examples of the Christian's sanctified life. With the Spirit's aid our words and actions can live out the love Christ gives to us—a love deep enough to send Him to the cross to win our forgiveness and eternal life.

It is a privilege to share God's Word, and a responsibility. We must carefully teach the pure Word of God. We need to apply it diligently to daily life in word and action. We may lead others to the cross, or become their stumbling block.

Ours is a dangerous profession. In some places in our world church workers can suffer physical danger at the hands of those who would thwart the Gospel message. Yet this is a temporal danger. A greater danger lies in leading others to err, to stray from God's true Word.

Remember the importance of your job. Recognize the responsibility you hold. And when you feel the weight of your job, feel also the upholding, guiding hand of your Savior. He walks with you every step of the way as your guard and guide. Rely on Him to lead you. Then the final evaluation of your job will be His word, "Well done, good and faithful servant."

Prayer
Dear Jesus, at times I am burdened by responsibility. Help me to be a true witness to You in word and action. Amen.

Activity
Thank another professional or volunteer for sharing your important responsibilities.

✛

Lacking Time

And God said, "Let there be light," and there
was light. God saw that the light was good, and
He separated the light from the darkness. God
called the light "day," and the darkness He called
"night." And there was evening, and there was
morning—the first day. Genesis 1:3–5

Day and night are set. Twenty-four hours make up a
day. But someone must have made a mistake. There
just aren't enough hours in the day. You've said it yourself, "There isn't enough time."

But God doesn't make mistakes. He created day
and night. He lovingly limited the hours of each day.
He gave us the marvelous gift of time. And when the
time was right, He sent His Son to bear the burden of
our sins on the cross, once, for all time! Why, then, do
we feel that time is so short? The days are too short?

We view things from our earthly perspective. We
list the things we want to accomplish. We know our
schedule. We know that there won't be time to accomplish all our plans. But for the Christian worker, even
time belongs to God. Even as we feel we are lacking
time, our God gives us time generously—the time to
accomplish what He wants. The time to do what He
has planned.

Rededicate your time to Him. Recognize that He can stretch hours and help us weed out activities that waste the gift of time.

When we feel frustrated with our lack of time, we can be assured that God has measured it out correctly and given it to us in planned amounts. We can ask His blessing upon the use of our time so that each day, each moment, each activity, will bring glory and praise to His name. Praise God that He always has time for us.

Prayer
Dear Heavenly Father, we know that You have not miscalculated our time. When we feel harried over rushed schedules, help us to turn each moment over to You so that it may be used wisely to Your glory. Thank You for being the Lord Eternal of all times. Amen.

Activity
Look at your schedule for today. How does your use of the day reflect Christ's lordship over your time?

✠

Priorities

*"The most important one," answered Jesus,
"is this: 'Hear, O Israel, the Lord our God, the
Lord is one. Love the Lord your God with all
your heart and with all your soul and with all
your mind and with all your strength.' The second is this: 'Love your neighbor as yourself.' "
Mark 12:29–31*

What comes first? How do you set priorities for daily
living? Some feel family and friends take first place.
Others place jobs in the number one time slot and
allow all other things to revolve around this choice.
Our God insists that He and He alone must be first
place. Loving Him with all our heart, soul, and mind
must be our first priority.

How do we set that priority? We don't. We simply reflect the all-encompassing love God shares with
us in His Son. Loving the Lord means setting time
aside for daily growth in God's Word. It means choos-
ing activities that are God-pleasing, that reflect God's
guides for daily living. It means coming together in
worship, service, and fellowship in response to His
invitation.

Then what comes in second place? The love of
neighbor. As Christian workers this priority seems easy
to achieve. It is our daily caring for those we serve. It

is the expansion of our Christian love to others outside the realm of our daily service. It means sharing the love of Christ in countless daily actions, from meal serving to tutoring. And in the times when we fail to see our neighbor's need, Christ calls us to reach out to everyone who needs His healing touch.

Setting priorities is no easy task. The world tries to pull at our commitment and encourages us to put ourselves first. It talks about personal needs and encourages the I'm-Number-1 syndrome. God's Holy Spirit serves as our constant companion and guide in keeping Christ first in our calendar setting, appointment making, and daily actions.

Christ's love for His neighbor motivated countless miracles and acts of service for those around Him. His love for His father and all people reached its height on Calvary. Through that selfless act He won us life and salvation.

Prayer
Lord, bless my schedule, my calendar, and my activity choices so that they reflect You first in my life and my love for my neighbor second. Amen.

Activity
Set aside 10 extra minutes today to read God's Word. Then do something special for a neighbor.

Give It All Up

Now a man came up to Jesus and asked, "Teacher, what good thing must I do to get eternal life?" . . . Jesus answered, "If you want to be perfect, go, sell your possessions and give to the poor, and you will have treasure in heaven. Then come, follow Me." Matthew 19:16, 21

Jesus exposed the heart of the young man's question. The young man felt confident about the commandments. He had kept those. But what was missing? Jesus answered knowingly, " . . . sell your possessions."

Possessions were standing in the young man's way. He could not give them up and look to Jesus as the Lord of his life.

Many marvel at Christians who leave home and family and go to far-off places to share the message of Christ. Others move to the inner city and give up lucrative positions in business to spread the Gospel message. All of us who follow may be called upon to sacrifice possessions, time, or popularity. Then the world says, "Look what they gave up."

Oh, that the young man in today's Bible reading had accepted Jesus' invitation. He would have given up possessions, but also so much more. In following Jesus Christians give up worry over sins. We know the peace that passes understanding. We know that Christ has taken away the guilt and despair that comes with the burden of sin. As followers of Christ, we give up fear of the future, for we know that God works in all things for our good. Christian disciples give up futility, for we know the purpose and direction Christ provides. Christians give up worry about death, for we know the sure hope of Christ's resurrection which wins us eternal life.

Oh, yes, what things we give up when we follow our Savior. What a joy to walk with Him in confidence daily! What a reason to share the message that He brings. Follow Him and rejoice over what you give up.

Prayer
Dear Jesus, when we follow You the world comments at the many things we give up. Help us to explain that we also give up guilt, despair, and eternal damnation. Thank You for the precious gifts won for us through Your life, death, and resurrection.

Activity
Make a list of the things you have gained as a follower of Christ.

✠

Use What You Have

Whoever has will be given more, and he will have an abundance. Whoever does not have, even what he has will be taken from him. Matthew 13:12

Think of it. It starts with a few scraps of material. Then patient hands piece them together. In time a beautiful pattern emerges. The scraps become a quilt that bears the care of one who can turn the pieces into beautiful perfection.

Much the same is true of our God. He blesses the individual talents that we offer in His service. Some raise their voices in praise to God. Others greet children on Sunday morning and share Jesus' love. Used talent and ability increase.

How sad the person who buries his or her talent. Much like the muscle that atrophies with disuse, the gifted Christians who bury their talent endanger its development and risk losing the gift.

Evaluate the many gifts that God has given you. What talents and abilities can you put into service for your Lord? When others compliment your talent, you can refer them to Jesus, the great giver of all gifts.

Do you have a talent that is getting rusty? Is there a gift that is begging to be put into service? Explore the possibilities today and ask God to open your eyes to ways to use them for Him. The God who gives you for-giveness and salvation through the atoning death and resurrection of the His Son will also give you the time and avenues to serve Him.

Prayer

Lord, help me to uncover the talents and abilities that I possess, and help me to put them into service in Your kingdom.

Activity

Review your talents and abilities and plan one new task using a gift that is getting rusty.

✛

Not the World's Wisdom

For the message of the cross is foolishness
to those who are perishing, but to us who are
being saved it is the power of God. For it is writ-
ten: "I will destroy the wisdom of the wise; the
intelligence of the intelligent I will frustrate."
1 Corinthians 1:18–19

Ads for job applicants often list needed credentials. Some list the level of education applicants must have in order to apply. Some list years of experience needed. Others list personal qualities helpful for success in that job. The Christian worker might see the word *wisdom* as part of his job requirements.

How does one measure wisdom? The world might equate this word with intelligence. We are all familiar with the world of written tests, personal evaluations, and records of day-to-day performance. At times our wisdom may fall short when measured with these standards.

Wisdom in God's eyes is readily accessible. The person who knows Jesus as Lord and Savior is truly wise. This simplicity often causes people to stumble. People look for something they can do. They look for a way to merit salvation. They want to earn their way to heaven, or at least feel that they have done a little something to get themselves there. The fact that eternal life is a free gift can cause some to stumble and search for a more complicated answer.

The Christian worker recognizes that free gift. He sings, "Nothing in my hands I bring, simply to the cross I cling." The cross brings wisdom. All who believe that Jesus is their Savior, who died on the cross to bring them forgiveness and eternal life, are truly wise. How sad that many who score high on intelligence tests score zero intelligence by God's standard.

May the wisdom of Christ be yours as you bring to the world God's simple plan for eternal life.

Prayer

Dear Lord, thank You for giving me the wise message of salvation in Jesus. Let me spread that message so others may share the wisdom and power of God. Amen.

Activity

Pick a wise saying from God's book of Proverbs as your thought for today.

⊕

A Reason for Boasting

Therefore, as it is written: "Let him who boasts boast in the Lord." 1 Corinthians 1:31

The mother brags about her child's achievements. The business man boasts of a new customer. The teacher boasts of record gains in scores. The grandmother pulls out her brag book. St. Paul gives another reason for boasting.

St. Paul is not saying that the Christian has no reason to feel personal worth. He is reminding us of the underlying source of worth that all Christians share. He is saying that it is not ability that gives worth, but the wonderful gift of God's Son, who thought us important enough to die for. It is Christ's sacrifice that gives us limitless value.

Now you truly have something to boast about. The very Son of God gave His life for you. The Lord of the universe gave up His heavenly home to come to earth to save you from eternal death. The God of life gave up His life that you might live forever.

Your Christian resumé is something to boast about. You have been redeemed by Christ the crucified. You can tell the world the value and meaning that His death and resurrection has given your life. Such boasting carries the wonderful message of salvation to the ends of the earth.

The Christian, then, does not boast about how great he is. Instead he boasts about how great his God is. No wonder the Christian sings "How Great Thou Art" with gusto. He daily realizes the greatness of His God in every moment of action of his life.

Prayer

Dear Lord, there is nothing in me that gives cause for boasting. I can merely boast in the greatness of my God who gave up His very Son for my salvation.

Activity

Think of the pages that would be included in a Christian's brag book.

✠

Only Servants

What, after all, is Apollos? And what is Paul?
Only servants, through whom you came to
believe—as the Lord has assigned to each his
task. I planted the seed, Apollos watered it, but
God made it grow. So neither he who plants nor
he who waters is anything, but only God, who
makes things grow. 1 Corinthians 3:5–7

Ranking one's importance is an ever-present temptation for church workers. Some would put the pastor
above the Sunday school teacher, the organist above
the custodian, the missionary above the social worker.
Today's Bible reference brings an equalizing message.
No one is greater than another. All are workers in the
kingdom. The adjective *great* belongs to God, who
brings growth.

Each fellow worker in the church is important and
purposeful. Each contributes to healthy growth in
God's kingdom.

Jesus Himself did not seek greatness. He humbled Himself to the point of death on the cross to pay
the price of our sins. He played the servant role and
washed His disciples' feet. He reminded us that the
greatest must be the least. By following His example,
we recognize the importance and worth of each member on Christ's team.

How would you write your job description? The word *servant* would state it concisely. In all our work for our Great Master, we know who brings growth and success. Our God is the One who causes people to come to know Jesus as their Lord and Savior.

We have no time to worry about greatness. We have a job to do. Our God blesses our work and brings growth to His kingdom. Time is limited. We go to work as servants in His kingdom.

Prayer
Thank You, Lord, for the variety of jobs in Your service. Let us each work with zeal and earnestness to bring Your saving message to the world.

Activity
Plan a team project with a fellow Christian worker.

✠

Someone for Everyone

Though I am free and belong to no man, I make myself a slave to everyone, to win as many as possible. To the Jews I became like a Jew, to win the Jews. To those under the law I became like one under the law (though I myself am not under the law), so as to win those under the law. To those not having the law I became like one not having the law (though I am not free from God's law but under Christ's law), so as to win those not having the law. To the weak I became weak, to win the weak. I have become all things to all men so that by all possible means I might save some. I do all this for the sake of the gospel, that I may share in its blessings. 1 Corinthians 9:19–23

Make a list of your hobbies. What type of travel interests you? What job do you do? What is your nationality or background? What type of car do you drive? Do you own pets? What are your favorite foods? The answers to these questions declare you a unique individual. "Uniqueness" is a valuable adjective in your job description as a Christian worker. In your distinctiveness you are able to minister and relate to particular groups of people. You can speak their language, understand their fears, and communicate effectively.

Paul used his uniqueness well. He became a slave to speak to slaves. He became like a Jew to speak with certainty and effectiveness to this group. He became weak to win the weak. Becoming "all things to all people" gave Paul multiple opportunities to spread Christ's message of life and salvation.

How have you used your uniqueness as a witnessing tool? How can you share the Good News that Christ gave His life for yours in a fresh way? Whom can you tell about Jesus as you share a hobby? What effect does your background have on faith sharing? How can you become all things to all people, so that you can save some through your proclamation of the Gospel message?

Prayer
Thank You, God, for making me a unique person. Let me find ways to minister to everyone with whom I come in contact so that I will be able to share with them the message that Christ died for all. Amen.

Activity
Display some part of a hobby or interest in your home or office. Find a way to use this display to give a hearing to the Gospel.

✠

No Look-Backs

Jesus replied, "No one who puts his hand to the plow and looks back is fit for service in the kingdom of God." Luke 9:62

If you played tag as a child, you probably remember the rule "No tag-backs." Once you were touched, you couldn't immediately tag the person who tagged you. A rule for the Christian's life of service might be "No look-backs."

God calls people into His service. He does not want us to look back to what we might have been or done. He calls us to look ahead to what things need to be accomplished as we use our talents to spread the message that Jesus is the Savior and only hope for life eternal. Jesus calls us to leave family and friends, to give up valuable economic gain in order to serve Him. He reminds us that anyone who loves father, mother, sister, or brother more than Him is not worthy to be His follower. Christ expects immediate and complete surrender to His way and will.

Jesus calls us to look forward. We have so many forward directions to pursue. We look forward to opportunities to share the message of salvation with those around us. We look forward to the joy of knowing that others will count heaven as their home because of us. We look forward to a joyful reunion with those who have come to know Jesus through the message we shared.

The devil calls, "Look back. See what you missed. Think of the treasures you could have had. Think of the worldly gain that could have been yours."

Jesus calls, "Look up. Remember the cross that saves. See the love that I have for you. See the home I have prepared for you."

No look-backs! Praise God for His call and the forward-looking direction He brings to your life.

Prayer
Thank You, God, that I have so much to look forward to. Thank You that my job is one that lasts forever. Help me to joyfully look ahead to service in Your kingdom. Amen.

Activity
Write a note of encouragement to someone who is tempted to look back.

⊕

It Will Come

But seek first His kingdom and His righ-
teousness, and all these things will be given to you
as well. Therefore do not worry about tomorrow,
for tomorrow will worry about itself. Each day
has enough trouble of its own. Matthew 6:33–34

It is often difficult to decide which things to put first. When we look at the advice of the world, we are tempted to put first things that give us security. We are tempted to worry about the future. We must save in order to be sure that we will always have enough to eat and drink. We plan for vacations, college, and our retirement years. When these things are settled, we are ready to get about the business of God's kingdom.

But God tells us to reverse our priorities. His kingdom comes first. We bring our gifts to Him first. He is first in all our planning and doing. And when our priorities are straight, marvelous things occur. All the things we need are added. God supplies our needs. He cares for us.

Often the time we could spend working for God is wasted in worrying about the future. God reminds us that when His kingdom takes first place in our lives, each day takes care of itself. The heavenly Father knows our needs and provides for them.

Christians might readily wear the sign "Don't worry. Be happy." We know that our worries are groundless. Our sins are forgiven. Our daily lives have purpose. Our future eternal home in heaven is secure because of our belief in Jesus as Savior and Redeemer.

Yes, it will all come. When Christ is in first place and kingdom-service is the number one priority, Christians experience the richness of daily life that comes from knowing Jesus. Christ's security system never fails.

Prayer
Dear Lord Jesus, when I am tempted to worry about the future, remind me that I can count on Your loving care. Let me know that You provide for me in every way. Amen.

Activity
Talk with a friend today about something you worried over needlessly. Share the message that God takes care of every need.

✠

Compelled

"Yet when I preach the gospel, I cannot boast, for I am compelled to preach. Woe to me if I do not preach the gospel!" 1 Corinthians 9:16

What things are you compelled to do? Some cannot leave the house for vacation without cleaning it first. Others cannot put down a book in the middle of a chapter. Some feel compelled to price an item at several stores before buying, while others feel compelled to buy only name-brands.

The Christian worker is also compelled. The word itself implies a kind of drive toward action. The Christian worker does not act for his own ends. He is not driven by a desperate need to be a super achiever, or to rank high in corporate achievements. The Christian worker is compelled rather to share the Gospel. God's Holy Spirit sparks an inner motivation and drive that makes this action the primary reason for his existence, even if his employment revolves around other tasks. Who can help but shout the joyful news that the weight of our sins has been lifted by Jesus Himself. His keeping of the Law and His death in our stead win us forgiveness and new life.

"Compelled to preach." What a wonderful phrase to describe the life, speech, and being of any Christian. This drive to share the Gospel motivates the Christian to actions which lead others to question "What makes this person stand out?" We share the wonderful news that our motivation comes from Jesus, our Lord and Savior.

The Gospel is the driving force in the life of every professional and volunteer Christian worker. One cannot but speak of the peace, hope, and joy that come from knowing the Lord.

What a blessing if others can describe you as "compelled to preach." Those words are the basis of our job description and the greatest comment on our life and work. Pray that you may be compelled to share Christ's Gospel, and that the Spirit may bring fruit to the message you share.

Prayer
Let me be compelled to speak the message of Your love in sending Jesus, my Savior, to earth to suffer and die for me. Let me never rest on what I have done, but continually see the need to share the powerful message of salvation. Amen.

Activity
Share the message of salvation with someone who has been on your heart and mind.

⊕

Sufferer

"To this you were called, because Christ suffered for you, leaving you an example, that you should follow in His steps." 1 Peter 2:21

Suffering can be found all over the world. Some suffer because of political injustice. Some suffer because their physical condition is deplorable. They live without shelter, warmth, proper clothing, or food. Still others suffer mental anguish over the loss of a loved one, the trauma of a broken relationship, or the burden of loneliness.

Christ has gone the way before us. Being very man, He knows the hurts that beset all of humanity. He knows the hurt of separation. He knows the pain of physical suffering. He knows the pain of bearing the weight of the world's sin on His shoulders.

Our Savior calls us to follow after Him. He calls us to follow His example. He demonstrates the loving, forgiving, understanding, and caring His Spirit sparks within us. Christ calls us, too, to follow His example in suffering. Our Savior obeyed His heavenly Father's will. He did not complain, but accepted the path set before Him. Even near the bitter end of His earthly life, His witness turned some of those around Him to acknowledge Him as Savior and Lord.

Follow Christ's example in your life. Ask for the strength and perseverance in suffering that only Christ can give. Rely on Him to buoy you up when suffering for His name's sake causes you grief and pain.

Prayer

Dear Lord Jesus, when I must suffer pain, humiliation, or rejection for Your Gospel's sake, give me the strength that comes from knowing that You have been there first. Amen.

Activity

Write a word of support for someone who is suffering for the sake of the Gospel.

✠

Footwasher

*"You call me 'Teacher' and 'Lord,' and rightly
so, for that is what I am. Now that I, your Lord
and Teacher, have washed your feet, you also
should wash one another's feet." John 13:13–14*

What image comes to mind when you picture our Lord
and Savior? Perhaps you think of Him as a great weatherman as He calms the stormy sea. Maybe His healing
qualities lead you to think of Him as a great physician.
Maybe His skill at meeting the needs, both physical
and spiritual, of His followers leads you to think of Him
as a great provider.

The most appropriate image of Jesus might be to
see Him in the role of footwasher. It is in this capacity
that Jesus promotes the role of every Christian worker
so we follow Jesus' example in providing needed service. Sometimes that service involves menial tasks,
even as Jesus bent low, drew water, and washed dirty,
smelly feet.

What job does Jesus lay before you that you consider unpleasant? When you find yourself regarding
some tasks beneath you, look to your Lord and Savior.
He humbled Himself to the point of death to pay the
price for your sin. His loving example will help you
bend low and serve Him in true humility.

Look around for feet to wash. It may be the care of an elderly friend, the building or refurbishing of a house in an inner-city neighborhood. It might mean serving on a mop-up crew at the church supper. Let your actions flow from a heart filled with the knowledge of Christ's greatest act of servitude—His death on Calvary's cross for you.

Prayer

Dear Jesus, let me serve as You have served. Open my eyes to see the needs of those around me and act in willing service. Amen.

Activity

What menial, servant tasks will you perform today? Let your attitude model Christ's attitude of service.

✠

Work That Lasts

If any man builds on this foundation using gold, silver, costly stones, wood, hay or straw, his work will be shown for what it is, because the Day will bring it to light. It will be revealed with fire, and the fire will test the quality of each man's work. 1 Corinthians 3:12–13

For five years the young husband and wife labored. They used days off, evenings, any extra hours, and every conceivable moment to refurbish, refinish, and renovate the old house. Then the job offer came and the young couple left the renovated house to the new owner. Only months later a fire destroyed their years of work. Nothing remained to give witness to their effort.

What lasts? A monument said to be immortal crumbles with rising flood waters. A life is shattered by the swiftness of a bullet. A successful business is destroyed by the competitor's strategies. So much of life is transient.

The writer of today's Bible section reminds us that our building in life will be put to the test. What can endure this testing? Faith built on Christ can survive the test of time and the trials that life brings. Christ kept the letter of the law for us. He felt every temptation we experience, yet never sinned. And after living a perfect life, He gave up His life to atone for our sins.

When one builds on Christ as Lord and Savior, all other things pale in comparison. This faith stands against the fiery darts that Satan would hurl to destroy it. Things built in accordance to God's will bring blessings and endure.

Many build with stone. They think that it is a substance that lasts forever. Some check to be sure that materials are fireproof. Others look for lifetime warranties. The worker that uses the material of the Gospel builds something that no one can destroy. It will stand the test of time and eternity.

Prayer
Lord, let me build on You. Let me seek Your will and ways as I lead others in Your church. Amen.

Activity
Compare occupations and list those which have products that last for a lifetime.

⊕

Just the Right Words

*"When you are brought before synagogues,
rulers and authorities, do not worry about how
you will defend yourselves or what you will say,
for the Holy Spirit will teach you at that time
what you should say." Luke 12:11–12*

All of us have groped for the right word. Perhaps we
have been in a situation that called for Christian witness. Maybe someone profaned our Lord's name and
we wanted to rise to His defense. Maybe a friend
expressed the futility of life and we wanted to share
Christ's plan and purpose. Perhaps a friend lost someone close and we knew the time was right to discuss
that colleague's relationship with Christ. What stops
us? What fears cross our mind?

Often we fear that we will not know just what to
say. What words should we use? Our Bible reading for
today gives us the answer. We can trust the Lord and
speak with boldness and confidence, for the Holy
Spirit will teach us at that time just what we should
say. He will give us words that accomplish the purpose
our gracious God has in mind.

When you are longing to reach out to someone in
need, Christ has done it for you. Describe peace that
comes from sins forgiven. Share the strength that
comes from knowing that your Savior is always with

you in life's most difficult situations. Communicate the joy you feel in knowing that you can count on heaven as your home.

The right words will come. God will bless your witness. Practice witnessing words with a fellow Christian. Pray for opportunities to use these words daily. Be assured that the Spirit will work with power as you witness and share the Gospel message.

Prayer
Dear Lord, let me see countless opportunities to witness in my daily life. Bless my words so they will accomplish Your will. Amen.

Activity
Practice telling the salvation story to a Christian friend so you are prepared to share it with someone who does not know its message.

✠

Find Another

Andrew, Simon Peter's brother, was one of the two who heard what John had said and who had followed Jesus. The first thing Andrew did was to find his brother Simon and tell him, "We have found the Messiah" (that is, the Christ). And he brought him to Jesus. John 1:40–42a

What's the first thing you do when you read about the greatest sale of the century? What do you do when you hear the good news that you have won some exciting contest? What happens when you receive word of a happy family event? You excitedly find someone to share the news. You want to tell someone what a great thing has happened in your life.

Andrew felt just that way. He had met the long-awaited Messiah. The prophecies he had learned from childhood were fulfilled in this one man. What a joy to know the waiting was over! God's plan was being worked out before his eyes. Life—new life—for him had just begun. But whom could he tell who would understand his excitement? It had to be Peter. Impetuous, outspoken Peter would be equally delighted to meet the Christ. So Andrew brought him; and Peter, too, received the call to follow Jesus.

We don't know much about Andrew. We hear of Peter on countless occasions. We sadly witness his denial. We listen to him express his deep love for the Master. We exult in his bold testimony that Jesus is the Christ. His Spirit-filled Pentecost message marks the birthday of the Christian church.

We do not know whom the Lord will call through us. We may be the Andrews who will bring more workers into Christ's kingdom.

You know the great news—Jesus the Christ has saved you from death and hell. Whom will you tell today?

Prayer

Lord, my heart is overflowing with the news that You are my Savior. Let me express it to someone today. Bless my words with Your Holy Spirit. Amen.

Activity

Write a letter to a family member. Be sure to speak to them about Christ.

Don't Turn Back

But Ruth replied, "Don't urge me to leave you or to turn back from you. Where you go I will go, and where you stay I will stay. Your people will be my people and your God my God. Where you die I will die, and there I will be buried. May the LORD deal with me, be it ever so severely, if anything but death separates you and me." Ruth 1:16–17

"When life gives you lemons, make lemonade." "When the going gets tough, the tough get going." How many more quotes like these can you name? These cheer-up words attempt to encourage us to stick it out and do the best with the difficult situation we face.

Ruth had known hunger. She had known what it was like to be separated from family members that she loved. She lived in a strange land. She had no children to comfort her. Her husband was dead, as were other male family members who could have provided for her. Yet she decided to follow her mother-in-law Naomi to a strange land and stick with the true God she had come to love.

Do you ever feel like just giving up? Is your job too hard? Is sharing Jesus in all situations too burdensome? God gives us Ruth as a heartening example. Her faithfulness in a difficult situation is not conjured up from her own stoic personality. This is faithfulness that stems from knowing God and relying on Him.

When she marries Boaz, she becomes part of the family whom God uses to bless all the world. Jesus is her descendent and our perfect example. He was never too tired to reach out in love to those who needed Him. He didn't say He'd already done enough when He was handed a cross. He willingly gave His life to save you! He willingly stands by you now to help you share His Gospel.

God will use you in mighty ways. You, too, will be a blessing to many as you spread God's marvelous salvation news.

Prayer
Dear Jesus, help me to share your love with all whose lives I touch. Amen.

Activity
Look at your family line. How many family members have been a blessing to the Christian church?

✤

You Were with Him

Now Peter was sitting out in the courtyard, and a servant girl came to him. "You also were with Jesus of Galilee," she said. But he denied it before them all. "I don't know what you're talking about," he said. Matthew 26:69–70

Guilt by association is a common problem in today's society. When drugs or alcohol are passed around, innocent people are sometimes convicted because they are in the wrong place at the wrong time. A chance remark may associate you with a specific political stance. Exit from a baseball stadium, and people will assume that you are a baseball fan.

The servant girl in today's Bible reading made an assumption about Peter. She assumed that Peter was a follower of Jesus because his accent gave him away.

Peter feared for his life. Jesus had just been led away by messengers of the high priest. Peter cursed and made every attempt to disassociate himself from His Lord and Savior. Then a rooster's crow brought him back to repentance.

What do others say about you? Do people associate you with your Lord and Savior? Have they seen you busily engaged in His work? Do they find you enjoying Bible study and worship experiences? Can people in your community identify you as a follower of Christ?

At times we, too, may share Peter's discomfort. We are not afraid of a crowd armed with swords, but we may fear ridicule over our church involvement. We may feel uncomfortable when people question us about our occupation or the number of hours we volunteer at church. We may sense people distancing themselves from us because of our relationship with Christ.

Our God calls us to repentance for the times we have denied Him or been poor witnesses for Him. He reminds us of the forgiveness that is ours and empowers us to be bold in our testimony of His greatness.

Prayer
Dear Jesus, let me count it a blessing that others know that I am one of Your followers. Help me use my Christian leadership as a way to alert my community to the greatness of Your forgiveness and love. Amen.

Activity
Examine your community involvement for chances to witness this week.

⊕

Who Do You Say He Is?

When Jesus came to the region of Caesarea Philippi, He asked His disciples, "Who do people say the Son of Man is?" They replied, "Some say John the Baptist; others say Elijah; and still others, Jeremiah or one of the prophets." "But what about you?" He asked. "Who do you say I am?" Simon Peter answered, "You are the Christ, the Son of the living God." Matthew 16:13–16

Hold up a picture of an individual and ask a crowd of people the question, "Who is this?" The answers may surprise you. Some may give the person's formal name. Others may call the person by a nickname. Some will not know him at all. Others might tell you about his job or other involvements. Some may identify him by the place where he lives and say, "He's my neighbor." Some will class him by their relationship to him and say, "He's my brother." A variety of people may know an individual in a variety of ways and roles.

Jesus held up Himself. He asked a telling question. "Who do people say the Son of Man is?" The answers varied. How would people today answer the very same question? Some people would call Jesus "teacher." They would cite His wise use of examples, discussion, and analogy. Others would call Him a good man and point out His healing miracles and His caring nature. Others would call Him scholar and point out His ability to quote the Old Testament.

Who do you say Jesus is? Perhaps the question annoys you. Of course you know who Jesus is, and you expect the people you work with to know Him as well. Yet, God calls us to know our answer and share it in our witness to others. Peter answered, "You are the Christ, the Son of the living God." We can boldly share that Jesus is *my* Lord, *my* Savior. He carried all the sins I have committed to the cross. He died to win me forgiveness and rose to win me new life with Him now on earth and an eternal home with Him in heaven. We can share the important difference He makes in our lives. Are those who know you best aware of your personal relationship with your Savior? Practice your personal answer to Jesus' question today.

Prayer
Dear Jesus, I want to witness to others that You are my personal Savior. Help me to tell them about the intimate relationship we share. Amen.

Activity
Write a letter to your spouse or child and describe your relationship with Jesus.

✠

A Dangerous Part

No man can tame the tongue. It is a restless evil, full of deadly poison. With the tongue we praise our Lord and Father, and with it we curse men, who have been made in God's likeness.
James 3:8–9

The same item; two purposes. The gun protects. The gun kills. We take the car on a pleasant vacation. We drive the car into an unescapable accident. A particular food satisfies a hungry person. The same food causes an allergic reaction in another individual.

The tongue works that way. It can be a blessing or a curse. The tongue can speak evil and ruin someone's reputation. It can speak words of hate and bring massive hurt and humiliation. It can set whole armies in motion. It can curse mankind and turn people away from Christ.

What a contrast the bridled Christian tongue makes! This tongue brings blessings through kind words. This tongue gives compliments that build up others. This tongue describes Christ's atoning work on the cross and says, "Jesus died and rose to save you." This tongue glorifies a marvelous Maker.

Time for a tongue check. How have you been using this most dangerous organ today? Did your words hurt or did they share the news of a glorious Savior? Bite your tongue against evil words and unbridle your tongue for Christian witness and praise.

Prayer

Lord, let me use my tongue to share Your message. Let the words from my mouth build up, encourage, and praise. Amen.

Activity

Tape record a conversation with your family or an individual or group with whom you work. Evaluate whether your tongue was used for good or evil.

⊕

Let's Hear It Again

When they heard about the resurrection of the dead, some of them sneered, but others said, "We want to hear You again on this subject." Acts 17:32

If you have read stories to small children you may have marveled at the number of times they will request the same story. Perhaps you have played a game five times, only to hear the words, "Let's play it again." Repetition and familiarity bring security and comfort. All of us like to hear the words "I love you" from a cherished person, even though we may hear that message countless times.

Sometimes it takes more than one hearing of a difficult message for us to really understand it. In our reading the let's-hear-it-again requests came from the council in Athens.

People will ask to hear God's Word again for a variety of reasons. Some want to hear it again because they love its message. The words give strength and security. The message of the Gospel can never be heard too frequently. Daily we rejoice in hearing the Good News that we lay our sins at the foot of the cross and receive the forgiveness won by Christ's sacrifice. The words of the old Gospel hymn ring true, "Those

93

who know it best are hungering and thirsting to hear it like the rest."

As Christian workers we must be constantly ready to repeat and explain God's Word. Some need time to let it work in their hearts with the Spirit's leading. They need time to gain understanding and insight into the great truths the Gospel reveals. The message of the Gospel is never trite or boring. It changes hearts and activates lives. It is the power of God for salvation.

Prayer
Lord, let me never tire of repeating Your Gospel words. Give me new excitement as I share Your loving message with all I meet. Amen.

Activity
Visit a member of your congregation who cannot attend church. Share a familiar section of Scripture such as Psalm 23. Observe this individual's reaction upon hearing this familiar message again.

⊕

Keep on Speaking

One night the Lord spoke to Paul in a vision: "Do not be afraid, keep on speaking, do not be silent. For I am with you, and no one is going to attack and harm you, because I have many people in this city." Acts 18:9–10

Newspaper headlines will quickly convince you that the world is evil. The bad news at times seems overwhelming. We Christians feel like throwing up our hands in despair. Our jobs seem futile. What direction should we take? What message should we bring? Is all our Christian witness to any avail? Maybe silence and self-preservation is the answer.

Paul must have faced similar disillusionment many times as he traveled on his missionary journeys. Not only did he confront evil, ignorance, and disbelief, he personally faced persecution, hatred, and physical danger. Silence would have been the easiest course of action.

But God meets the needs of those who love and serve Him. In a very real way God came to Paul to tell him that he should not give up. Paul need not fear. God's protection is greater than any danger. He should continue to teach the Word of God.

God echoes that message to us. He tells us to "keep on speaking." We need to keep sharing the

Gospel message with a world that needs constant reminders of the love and goodness of our God. Forgiveness, peace, and life eternal can only come through sharing what our Savior has done for us.

Practice ignoring Quiet-Please signs. God's message to us today is quite the opposite. Keep speaking. God wants us to constantly proclaim His Gospel until all the world is speaking it as well.

Prayer
Dear Jesus, keep me speaking the words that bring life and salvation to a world entrenched with sin. Let Your words be on my lips. Let me find countless ways to share Your message. Amen.

Activity
Write a note reading "Keep speaking," and place it on your desk or table as a reminder of your charge to speak the message of Jesus.

✠

A Place to Witness

About midnight Paul and Silas were praying and singing hymns to God, and the other prisoners were listening to them. Acts 16:25

Where is the best place to share Christ? It would be interesting to create a photo essay on places to witness. Some would think of majestic cathedrals in Europe. Others would envision people on doorsteps. Still others might focus on a remote African village. Where is your place to share the message of your Savior, Jesus Christ?

Paul's missionary journeys had led him to a variety of cities and circumstances. Today's text finds Paul and Silas witnessing in prison. In the confines of a dark Roman prison, Paul and Silas were empowered to sing hymns and pray to God. And God tells us that "the other prisoners were listening to them."

Where is the best place to share Christ? Wherever you work, socialize, and speak. The world is our arena for witness. We can use hobbies, business, and interests to give us a place to share the cross.

Paul's witness accomplished God's purpose. God's Holy Spirit brought the jailer and his family to saving faith. Perhaps God will use your prayer in a restaurant, or your words on an airplane, as His Spirit's tool.

Our society is a global one. People travel the world for business and pleasure. Our society is a desperate one. Never has the Gospel message been needed more critically. Pray God for countless places to witness for Him. Ask His Spirit to make you ready at a moment's notice to proclaim the message that Christ lived a perfect life for you, paid the price of your sins, and won you a glorious home in heaven. Open your eyes to see new opportunities every day to speak a message of His truth.

Prayer

Dear God, the world offers countless places for witness. Make me alert to these opportunities so that others will hear the message of the place in heaven You have prepared for them. Amen.

Activity

Make a list of your day's activities. Pray about ways to witness your faith in your Savior at each location.

✠

Mountaintop Experiences

*Peter said to Jesus, "Rabbi, it is good for us
to be here. Let us put up three shelters—one for
You, one for Moses and one for Elijah." Mark 9:5*

The music was terrific. The choir gave you chills.
When you sang, you felt an unexplainable joy. The
message from God's Word thrilled you. You experienced a feeling of fellowship with those around you.
The Sacrament seemed like a true "foretaste of the
feast divine." Then came the benediction. In your
heart you echoed the words of Peter, "It is good for us
to be here." Perhaps you, too, wished that you could
pitch your tent and stay. How wonderful to feel this
excitement and closeness to your God and your Christian family! But then came the recessional. It was time
to move out and you did so reluctantly.

Wonderful moments of high feeling and emotion
excite the life of every child of God. But the world
calls. Life goes on and we must leave the mountaintop
experiences to launch into the daily life down on the
plain. Those on the plain need to hear our message.
They need to hear of a joy that keeps on going when
life's trials and troubles surround. They need to know
that Jesus experienced the trials and heartaches they
feel and laid down His life to atone for their sins. A

place in heaven is prepared for them as they rely on that saving message.

Store the mountaintop experiences in your memory. Let them feed you and restore you when the battle on the plain gets fierce and draining. Your gracious God is with you on the mountaintop and the plain.

Prayer

Dear Lord, thank You for the joyful experiences that build me up. Thank You for worship and faith experiences that move me to share Your good news. Let them buoy me up when the daily blahs drag me down. Amen.

Activity

Write a letter to a friend who is suffering on the plain. Remind your friend of God's power and presence in this circumstance.

✠

What I Have

*Then Peter said, "Silver or gold I do not have,
but what I have I give you. In the name of Jesus
Christ of Nazareth, walk." Acts 3:6*

No doubt you have experienced the emotion Peter
might have felt as he looked upon the need of the crippled man. You feel it when you see the man on the side
of the road carrying a sign that says, "Will work for
food." Or maybe it is the cry for help in a faraway country. Or when you read a newspaper ad urging you to
provide a home for a needy child. Perhaps you have
been torn between the desire to help and the knowledge that your financial resources are limited.

But a Christian worker can put aside the feelings
of limited funds and inadequate means with joy. We
can say with Peter, "What I have I give you." We give
from the richness of the blessings God has given us.
We share our mites to feed the hungry. We donate
time, talent, and what treasure we can to meet the
needs of those around us.

In the miracle recorded in Acts, healing wasn't the
best gift Peter gave the crippled man. What Peter had
in abundant measure was the wonderful message of
Jesus Christ. He performed the miracle in the name
of that Savior, and it was that Savior who filled the crippled man's greatest need. Yes, it was a wonder to see

him leap with joy and praise God. It is an equally great wonder to see those crippled by sin arise with sins forgiven to walk in the ways Christ directs.

We do have something to give. It is the greatest gift of all time. We can shout it out and share all that we have—the good news of our Savior, Jesus Christ. Think about it today. See the sin-crippled and sin-blinded, deaf to the message, and pray for Spirit-given opportunities to share God's plan for salvation in Jesus Christ. When you share this message, God may grant the greatest gifts of all—sins forgiven, peace for daily living, and the sure hope of life eternal.

Prayer
Dear heavenly Father, sometimes I feel frustrated that I cannot meet the physical needs of those all around me. Help me to remember that I can bring to many the greatest gift, the message of salvation. Let me be filled with the joy that sharing that message brings. Amen.

Activity
Make a special effort to share the message of Jesus with one person today.

✠

Always Rejoicing

Rejoice in the Lord always. I will say it again:
Rejoice! Philippians 4:4

Children enjoy an art form called crayon etching. They color a paper with splotches of bright color, then cover the entire page with heavy, black crayon. When they draw with a pointed object, the black is scratched away to reveal their etching in bright colors.

The Christian life is much like this simple art technique. The joy of knowing Christ as our Savior undergirds everything. It breaks through the dark periods that pervade our lives. It is in the bold, happy moments of life when being a Christian seems an easy task. It is there also under the dark, heavy moments of life, when the ache of loneliness, death, sin, and disease try to rob us of happiness. As Christians we can rejoice even when the world around calls us to despair.

Jesus is the Savior and Lord of our lives. When the world would coax and lure us to be sorrowful and give up, Jesus' cross brings sure and certain hope. Christ is with us in the trials of life, guiding us to what is eternally best for us.

We will find ourselves many times in times of trial looking to the promises of God for the reason for underlying joy. Those promises stand sure. Through graveside tears we can boldly proclaim, "I know that my Redeemer lives." When traveling, we remember Christ's words, "Lo, I am with you always." When life takes unexpected turns, we can cheerfully say, "All things work together for good . . . ."

What is your emotional state today? Are you exuberantly joyful or dreadfully sad? May God's messages of salvation and promise be your emotional support as you realize peace and joy from your Savior, Jesus Christ.

Prayer

Dear Jesus, at times it seems impossible to rejoice always. Yet underneath even the saddest times of daily life, the comfort of Your forgiveness and love brings me a joy that sustains me. Constantly remind me of that joy when the world would try to take it away. Amen.

Activity

Provide some unexpected joy to a shut-in friend. Be sure to include a Christian message about the true joy of life in Christ Jesus.

⊕

A Reason for Joy

"Rejoice with me; I have found my lost sheep." Luke 15:6

What makes you rejoice? It may be the birth of a child. It might be good news on the job. Perhaps it is a vacation or good news from a child. Countless things in life bring us joy. Then we look heavenward and bless a gracious and loving God.

Christ, too, rejoices. His joy comes whenever He finds a lost sheep. He rejoices over one sinner who repents. That event motivates the angels to exclaim and our God to smile.

We, too, rejoice at such an event. We rejoice to see the child brought by loving parents and enfolded through Baptism into Christ's kingdom. We watch the penitent sinners rise from Christ's table renewed and restored, and there is joy. We confess our sins and experience the joy that absolution brings.

Someone has said that joy is multiplied as it is given away. So many worldly joys last just a moment. So many joys are self-centered. How different the joy of a sinner who becomes a child of God. This joy lasts for all eternity, as a new member of Christ's family enters an eternal relationship.

We help create times of joy when we share the message of salvation with those around us. We help give the Spirit the opportunity to work in the lives of a sinner and bring the turnaround which works faith and true joy.

Let heaven rejoice. Let the angels be glad. Share your joy in salvation with someone else today. Be the map for the lost. Share direction with the wandering. Jesus is the Way. He alone is the Truth and the Life. Only through Him can we know forgiveness, life, joy, and salvation.

Prayer
Dear heavenly Father, how wonderful to know that we share in the joy of a lost sinner brought to salvation. Help me to share that good news so that others may know the true joy that comes from living as Your child. Amen.

Activity
Use a tract or a piece of Christian jewelry as a tool to share your joy in Christ with someone today.

⊕

Morning

For His anger lasts only a moment, but His favor lasts a lifetime; weeping may remain for a night, but rejoicing comes in the morning. Psalm 30:5

If you know a morning person, you can understand the concept behind this verse. The true morning person often finds working at night tiring and frustrating. At night, problems seem complex and insurmountable. But to the morning person, this frustration is as brief as the house guests who only come for a one-night stay. In the morning they are on their way. So are the tears and sadness that night can bring.

For many, the morning is a time of rejoicing. Think of the last time you had difficulty sleeping. Remember the relief of seeing the morning light and realizing you finally fell into restful sleep. Have you ever waited through the night with a loved one in critical condition? Somehow making it until the morning seems to bring hope.

God's anger is brief—as brief as the visit of the guest who just stays one night. His favor is forever. God favored us by giving up the life of His only Son. Surely no favor or love is greater than that.

We may feel for a moment the sting of sin. But then comes the morning of rejoicing. The Gospel speaks to us forgiveness. God tells us that, in Jesus, sin is no longer charged to our account. We are forgiven, redeemed, restored and heavenward bound. What joy and rejoicing is ours!

Prayer

Dear Jesus, help me to know the joy of a new day. Help me to delight in my salvation. Let this joy well up in me and spill over to others. Amen.

Activity

Write the word "rejoice" on a card. Place it where you will see it first thing in the morning to remind you that the mercies of God are new to you each day.

✠

Walking in the Truth

It gave me great joy to have some brothers
come and tell about your faithfulness to the truth
and how you continue to walk in the truth. I have
no greater joy than to hear that my children are
walking in the truth. 3 John 3–4

There are many ways and reasons to walk in today's society. There are walks of protest. People carry placards and shout slogans to express their opposition to some policy or person. There are walks for various charities where people sponsor walkers and make donations to various causes. There are exercise walks where walkers strive to achieve pace and distance to keep physically fit.

The walk in today's Bible reading is one that is always positive and always brings joy. John is rejoicing to hear that those with whom he has shared Christ's Gospel message are "walking in the truth."

What does it mean to "walk in the truth"? This is no physical march along the highways of life. To walk in truth means to follow along the ways that are set out clearly in God's Word. Following the only "Way," Jesus, and walking in His way is a wonderful way to step.

Our God wants us to know His way. Walking after Jesus leads us to forgiveness, renewal, and everlasting life. Jesus' walk leads us to paths of service and calls us to share the truth that He is Lord and Savior with all along the way.

When those of us who are Christian leaders hear the word that those we have schooled in the truth are staying on that path, we feel a great joy. We rejoice that the Spirit is alive within them and that they have continued on the right path.

Think of those you serve. Whom can you count as "walking in the truth"? What examples of faithfulness have you heard this week? Praise God that you can share in the joy that walking together in Christ's way brings.

Prayer

Thank You, heavenly Father, for those who walk in the truth. Keep those I have taught close to You. Amen.

Activity

Take a walk and mentally thank God for people whose life in Christ makes you rejoice.

✛

A Turn to Joy

"Are you asking one another what I meant when I said, 'In a little while you will see me no more, and then after a little while you will see me'? I tell you the truth, you will weep and mourn while the world rejoices. You will grieve, but your grief will turn to joy." John 16:19–20

You've watched it happen. A child plays happily beside its parents. The nurse calls a name. The parents take the child to the small, sterile cubicle. The child smiles and then—the nurse administers the shot. A loud wail is heard. Tears fall quickly. The nurse holds out a lollipop, and all is happiness again. The former joy and smile return.

The disciples did not fully comprehend what was happening as Jesus moved toward Calvary. Jesus would leave them. That message in itself was enough to bring sadness. They had traveled with the Master. They had seen the healing touch of His caring hands. They had come to learn so many things about the heavenly Father from His teaching. How was it possible that they would not see Him for awhile, and then see Him again?

Yes, Jesus' death brought sorrow to His followers. But how temporary their grief when compared to their Easter joy. How temporary their grief compared to the eternal home Christ won for them in heaven.

For us too, daily sorrows and discouragements are temporary. Yet God can use them to lead us to the cross—to remind us of just what happened when He sacrificed the life of His Son to win us forgiveness and life. Even severe sorrows are short in duration compared to the "turn to joy" that will be ours in heaven. What joy will be ours as we meet our Savior face to face! That message brings joy that cannot be diminished even in the midst of daily frustrations.

Prayer
Dear Jesus, I rejoice that I will see You again in heaven. Let this message give perspective to moments of earthly sadness. Amen.

Activity
Write a message of Christian understanding to someone who has recently experienced the death of a loved one. You might share the verse for today's meditation.

Pure Joy

Consider it pure joy, my brothers, whenever you face trials of many kinds, because you know that the testing of your faith develops perseverance. Perseverance must finish its work so that you may be mature and complete, not lacking anything. James 1:2–4

A certain bath soap advertises that it is 99 and ⁴⁴⁄₁₀₀ percent pure. The kind of joy our text for today talks about beats even that percentage. It is hard to think of joy when one is facing trials, but James explains how that is possible for the Christian. We know that God can use our troubles to refine our faith and help us develop perseverance.

Much in life needs refinement to be all it can be. The first draft of a book is nothing compared to the perfected end piece. Raw gold ore is no thing of beauty compared to the refined product of pure gold.

A Christian can see purpose in suffering. When enduring trials, the Christian knows God is making something beautiful out of what seems perverse and difficult.

God gave His best in giving us the gift of His Son Jesus Christ to atone for our imperfections. He gives us His best in the daily working out of our lives. Even in suffering we can rejoice because we know our sins are forgiven. We can rejoice because we know that God is with us, supporting us each step of the way. We can rejoice because we know with certainty that we look forward to life eternal with Him.

Prayer

Dear Lord, sometimes it is hard to feel joy in times of difficulty. Boost me up by reminding me that You always work for my good. Amen.

Activity

Write the word "perseverance" on your planning calendar.

⊕

Because of You

They only heard the report: "The man who formerly persecuted us is now preaching the faith he once tried to destroy." And they praised God because of me. Galatians 1:23–24

Compliments make our day. We like to hear that we are doing something well and that people appreciate our efforts. Think of the last genuine compliment you received and the feelings that accompanied it. No doubt Paul felt uplifted as he heard the message from the churches where he had labored. They were involved in Christ. They had come to know Jesus as their Savior. They were part of the company of believers that was expanding throughout the world.

The comment from these churches is one that no doubt lifted Paul's spirits. What joy Paul must have felt as he recognized that others were praising God because of the message of salvation that they had heard from him.

Who is praising God today because of you? No doubt you can think of countless people with whom you have shared the glorious Gospel message. Thank God for this privilege. Thank God that others can experience the love and forgiveness that are part of your everyday reason to rejoice. Thank God that there will be those in heaven who point to you as the one who shared that life-giving message.

But your work is not done. Look around you and you will see a world needing that wonderful message. Many do not know that Jesus is the Way, the Truth, and the Life. Pray that God will use you mightily to spread that Word. Pray that many others will have reason to bless God because of you and the saving message you bring to their life.

Prayer

Dear Jesus, it is with joy that I bless You for the privilege of sharing Your message with others. Let the word that I share bring joy and salvation to many who do not know You. Amen.

Activity

Write a note to someone who has shared Christ with you. Explain that you are praising God because of that witness.

✠

Burden Carriers

Carry each other's burdens, and in this way
you will fulfill the law of Christ. Galatians 6:2

Recently my husband had knee surgery. The three days of recuperation turned into four weeks. One great frustration for him was that he couldn't carry anything while using crutches. He needed help to carry a cup of coffee to the office, pick up the mail, or take along a book. He had to find a "burden bearer." And it was hard for him to admit that he needed help to do such a simple task.

All of us like to be self-reliant. We like to think that we can handle things on our own. But then reality sets in and we know we cannot go it on our own. We must allow others to help us bear our burdens, as we share in theirs. We constantly exchange roles as we bear burdens and have our burdens borne.

Fellow Christians share each other's hurts. We offer words of comfort and strength to each other. We organize a carpool, share a meal, baby-sit for a neighbor, or visit a lonely friend. We lift each other up with God's promises that bring strength, empowerment, life. We can also be gracious receivers as others serve us as "little Christs" and bear our burdens.

Best of all, as Christians bearing each others burdens, we lay our burdens on Christ's shoulders and together know that He can lift them and give us relief. How sad that we often try to "go it alone," rather than going to Him.

Most of all, as Christian burden-bearers we can remind each other that our greatest burden has already been removed. Our sins have been taken away. Our fear of death is unfounded. Our worry about eternity is replaced with our Savior's promise of forgiveness, strength, and eternal life.

Think of a burden you are bearing. Share it with a Christian friend. Together, turn your burden over to your Savior.

Prayer
Dear Lord, help me to be willing to bear my brothers' and sisters' burdens. And help me turn over the weight of my burdens to You. Amen.

Activity
Bring some relief to a load someone is carrying.

⟊

Growing Up

*Then we will no longer be infants, tossed
back and forth by the waves, and blown here and
there by every wind of teaching and by the cunning and craftiness of men in their deceitful
scheming. Instead, speaking the truth in love, we
will in all things grow up into Him who is the
Head, that is, Christ. Ephesians 4:14–15*

Usually when we speak of growing up we are suggest-
ing that someone act more thoughtfully and maturely.
We encourage this person to be responsible and reliable.

God encourages us to "grow-up." He calls us to
grow in maturity through His Word. Clearly knowing
what our God teaches brings stability to our lives. His
Spirit is our teacher. God's Word clearly tells us how
God sacrificed the life of His Son to win our salvation.
When the Spirit guides this type of study, we are not
easily led astray or deceived by those who would
attempt to pull us away from our faith in Jesus as our
Lord and Savior.

Growing up as a Christian involves following the
Spirit's lead in our work and commitment. It involves
personal Bible study, group Bible study, worship, and
prayer. It involves charting a clear course of daily living
with Christ as pilot, compass, and anchor. With Christ

in control we will not be blown off the course of Christian growing.

Growing as a Christian involves Spirit-given commitment to learning more each day. We will not graduate until the Lord calls us home. As we study together with fellow Christians, we are naturally drawn together in service, and teamwork develops. Differences disappear as we realize the common nature of our purpose. Love of Jesus bonds us with our colleagues in His service.

Prayer
Dear Jesus, help me to grow up in You. Remind me that this growing never ends. Let me count on the food of Your Word as essential to that growth. Amen.

Activity
Display a growth chart with suggested Bible readings in an area where you and fellow Christian workers can see it and take time to read the passages.

☩

Without Complaining or Arguing

*Do everything without complaining or argu-
ing, so that you may become blameless and pure,
children of God without fault in a crooked and
depraved generation, in which you shine like
stars in the universe as you hold out the word of
life. Philippians 2:14–16a*

Western states whose skylines are devoid of skyscrap-
ers take pride in being called big-sky country. On a
clear night in big-sky country one cannot help but marvel at the beauty of God's creation. The stars shine
clearly and there seem to be countless numbers more
than a city view permits.

God calls us to shine like stars. What a tall order!
We can only do it with the help of the in-dwelling
Christ. He shone with God's love as He obeyed His
Father's will and paid for our sins to win us forgiveness.
When facing this sacrifice, the Spirit helps us empty
ourselves of selfish will and seek God's will. We place
the betterment of others before self. We do the most
menial task willingly, as if doing it for Christ.

God often uses the words "cheerful, gracious, and
willing" to describe the attitudes of those who would

work for Him. They call for a different attitude than one who attacks a task with, "Well, if I *have* to."

Look around you for the stars of Christian service. The Holy Spirit brought them to faith. They sparkle with activity done willingly in His service. They volunteer before they are asked. They accomplish difficult tasks with cheerfulness and cooperation, knowing it is Christ who works in them.

Attitudes of agreement and cheerfulness are blessings from God. They are fruits of the Spirit patterned after the willingness with which Christ went to Calvary. Sparkling Christian stars blessed with these attitudes look on service as a privilege, for they know the Christ who came not to be served but to serve.

Prayer

Lord, let my service to You shine like a star as I work cheerfully and agreeably in Your kingdom. Amen.

Activity

Write today's Bible verse on a star and give it to someone who has willingly done a task of Christian service for you.

⊕

Perfect Unity

*Therefore, as God's chosen people, holy and
dearly loved, clothe yourselves with compassion,
kindness, humility, gentleness and patience. Bear
with each other and forgive whatever grievances
you may have against one another. Forgive as the
Lord forgave you. And over all these virtues put
on love, which binds them all together in perfect
unity. Colossians 3:12–14*

Many things unite people. Sometimes people are
united by their love of a sport. At other times family
blood ties unite a rather different group of individuals. At other times love for a particular type of music
unites people. Take a moment to think of things in your
life which unite you with others.

In our Bible reading for today St. Paul reminds
us of Christian virtues which unite members of Christ's
kingdom as they work together. Compassion, kindness,
gentleness, and patience are the oil that lubricates daily
Christian life. Forgiveness deletes grudges and promotes a healing spirit. When these qualities are lacking, friction, hatred, and arguing quickly set in.

Love is the greatest virtue to aid the smoothly
working Christian group. In others of his epistles, Paul
clearly defines this word. Love wants the best for others. Love protects, trusts, hopes, perseveres. Love is

not easily angered, nor does it keep a record of wrongs. Love sent Jesus to the cross. God's love freely forgives us because of the sacrifice His Son made there. No wonder love is the great unifier as Christians work together.

Christians who know clearly the love of their Savior are empowered by the Spirit to display this loving attitude in return. Christians who realize the limitless and constant love of Christ model that love in their dealings with others.

Prayer
Dear Holy Spirit, fill me with the love of Jesus that I may display true Christian love to my fellow workers today. Amen.

Activity
Surprise a fellow worker with an act of love today.

⊕

Watch the Payback

Make sure that nobody pays back wrong for wrong, but always try to be kind to each other and to everyone else. 1 Thessalonians 5:15

In today's world people are quick to pay back. If the car ahead of you cuts in too short, retribution is expected. When children play, a slap from one may bring a quick slap back from the other. Angry words often get paid back with more angry words.

Our God encourages paybacks, but not in kind. When someone does evil to us, God directs us to pay them back with kindness. Think of the last time you were wronged. Can you imagine turning around and doing a kind and loving deed for the person who wronged you? Unbelievable!

Jesus gave the perfect example. When soldiers arrested Him, Peter cut off the ear of the high priest's servant. Jesus repaid his captors with the kindness of healing. How surprised they must have been! What a model for perfect payback—kindness for contempt.

As Jesus hung on the cross, He did not withhold the benefits of the cross from His tormentors. Instead God's Word records clearly, "He died for all." Those who treated Him with scorn, mockery, and hatred were the very ones He came to save. He paid back the evil that surrounded Him with the greatest good—the gift of forgiveness and everlasting life.

What ill are you harboring against someone? Which broken relationships are dragging you down today? Our God tells you how to handle these situations. Begin with yourself. Begin with forgiveness and a payback modeled after Christ's. He shows us how to repay evil and hurt with good. This is the power for healing that the indwelling Christ brings to our lives.

Prayer
Dear Jesus, sometimes my relationships get strained and hurtful. Then I count the hurt and look for ways to pay it back. Give me the power of Your Holy Spirit to pay back evil with good. Amen.

Activity
Pay back some unkindness with kindness today.

⊕

All His Parts

*Now you are the body of Christ, and each
one of you is a part of it. 1 Corinthians 12:27*

If you ever put together a puzzle and were missing one piece, you know the frustration of a missing part. A missing piece makes the picture incomplete. A missing piece detracts from the beauty of the whole.

Each Christian is also an important piece—a piece of the body of Christ. In Paul's model each part of the body works together in delicate balance. When one part malfunctions, other parts are unable to do their work properly.

We are a part of the body of Christ. Without our contributions and the proper functioning of our part, the body cannot live, move, and grow effectively. Our contribution is vital to the life of the Christian church.

The poison of sin cripples the body of Christ. This poison may cause one part of the body to think itself more important than another. It may harm a body part so that it cannot operate properly. It may cause bickering and strife and throw the body out of balance.

But there is an antidote for the poison of sin. The cure comes from the Great Physician. He gets the body functioning through the forgiveness and life that He alone can bring. He reminds us that each part of the body was important enough to die for. He gave His precious life to cut out sin's cancer and bring new life to all who believe in Him.

Call on your Savior for healing. Ask Him to make each part of His body run smoothly and effectively to accomplish His purposes. Let the Spirit guide you to serve in ways that bring praise and glory to Christ's body, the church.

Prayer

Dear Great Physician, remind me that I need Your power and forgiveness to work together smoothly as part of the body of Christ. Give me the healing that You alone can give. Remind me of the importance of each part as we work together for You. Amen.

Activity

Write a note to one part of your Christian body and express thanks for the way you work together.

✛

Devoted

*They devoted themselves to the apostles'
teaching, and to the fellowship, to the breaking of
bread and to prayer. Acts 2:42*

How would others describe your Christian team of
workers? What adjectives might be used? Make a list
of the words you would use to describe your Christian
team.

The writer of Acts characterized the early Christians by their devotion. That word carries feelings of
affection, loyalty, and faithfulness. The followers
devoted themselves to the apostles' teaching, to fellowship, and to the breaking of bread and prayer. If
we could have seen them involved in these actions, no
doubt we would have recognized the marks of Christians working and growing together.

How do others see your Christian team? To what
are you devoted? What jobs command your loyalty,
faithfulness, and affection? Think of the positive
aspects of your team. Together you have a common
Savior, Jesus Christ. You rejoice in His gift of forgiveness. You share the purpose of proclaiming Christ to
the world. You share the eternal vision of heaven as
your home. You recognize that there is more to life
than the present frustrations, anxieties, and discouragements. You know that Christ's love brings support

and vision for the future when eternal happiness and living face-to-face with Him are yours.

If your team is devoted to Christ's teaching, fellowship, the breaking of bread, and prayer, you can be sure that Christ is in your midst to bless your purpose and plans. Where these marks are lacking, God offers forgiveness and the empowerment of His Holy Spirit to give healing and purpose to the Christian team. Check your word list again. What new words would you like to add, with the Spirit's guidance?

Prayer

Dear Lord, bless those of us who work together to serve You. Let us be devoted to Your teachings and to the Christian fellowship, the sacraments, and prayer. Let Your forgiveness bring healing where we have failed. Give us a sense of the mission we share in Christ Jesus. Amen.

Activity

Plan a fellowship activity for your Christian team.

✠

Hand-Holders

*So Joshua fought the Amalekites as Moses
had ordered, and Moses, Aaron and Hur went to
the top of the hill. As long as Moses held up his
hands, the Israelites were winning, but whenever
he lowered his hands, the Amalekites were winning. When Moses' hands grew tired, they took a
stone and put it under him and he sat on it.
Aaron and Hur held his hands up—one on one
side, one on the other—so that his hands remained steady till sunset. Exodus 17:10–12*

Holding hands is a sign of affection. It binds two people together and shows others their common bond.
The hand holding in today's Bible section goes a step
further. Aaron and Hur's supporting of Moses' hands
gave the Israelites an important victory. An undergird-
ing of strength marked their support.

Whose hands are you holding? Many members
among Christ's workers need your support today. Our
Christian missionaries need to know that, although
they are often alone physically in their mission, they
are never really alone. We pray for them. We send let-
ters of encouragement. We hold their hands.

Christian workers struggle through difficult times
daily. Sometimes the people they serve may not be
receptive to the message of God's Word. They may dis-

like the messenger because of the message, and even cause problems and hurt feelings. Fellow workers need to be hand holders as they speak words of encouragement and give support.

Hand-holding can be tiring. It can even bring personal discomfort. To gain motivation for this task we need only to look at our Savior's hands. Those hands, nailed to the cross and lifted in blessing, give us strength and support for all the times of life. Christ's hands work through the hands of fellow Christians in His service. We can support each other because our Savior opens His hands to give us forgiveness, love, and life eternal.

Prayer

Dear Savior, help me to support my fellow workers and hold their hands in the difficult moments of life. Let me picture the image of your nail-scarred hands to motivate my support for each member of my Christian team. Amen.

Activity

Trace around your hand. On it, write a supporting compliment for a fellow Christian worker.

✠

Center of Forgiveness

Be kind and compassionate to one another, forgiving each other, just as in Christ God forgave you. Ephesians 4:32

All golf balls may look the same to some people, but a golf pro recognizes their vast differences. The core of a golf ball makes it unique. The core may be solid, or filled with water or some other type of liquid. To the progolfer, the core makes a difference.

The core also makes a difference for Christians working together. And the solid core for Christians working together is forgiveness. This forgiveness gives the Christian community a distinctiveness that makes it stand out among other groups of workers.

Christians—when relying on the Spirit's guidance—do not keep a record of wrongs. They do not hold grudges or rejoice at the wrongs of others. Christians draw on their core—forgiveness. They put the past with its wrongs behind and forge ahead. Personal hurts are salved with the healing that forgiveness brings. They act out forgiveness by proceeding as if nothing happened—for when forgiveness is applied, the past is eliminated.

God models for us the marvelous core of forgiveness behavior. He does this through His unconditional forgiveness of us. Because of the redeeming sacrifice of His Son, He does not hold sin to our account. He forgives fully and freely. No sin is too great that it can't be covered by His boundless forgiveness.

When we look at ourselves critically, we recognize fully the great need for Christ's forgiveness. We see broken promises, weak faith, failure to act in God-pleasing ways. We have been forgiven much. With the power of the Holy Spirit we can emulate Christ's forgiveness to others. We can pour out Christian forgiveness to those who have wronged us and move forward in the work Christ would have us do.

Prayer
Dear Savior, let forgiveness be the core of my dealings with others. Give me Your Holy Spirit so that I may model the forgiveness that You have so freely given me. Amen.

Activity
If you have difficulties with a fellow worker, exercise your core of forgiveness today.

✠

He Did It First

> *We love because He first loved us. If anyone*
> *says, "I love God," yet hates his brother, he is a*
> *liar. For anyone who does not love his brother,*
> *whom he has seen, cannot love God, whom he*
> *has not seen. And He has given us this command:*
> *Whoever loves God must also love his brother.*
> *1 John 4:19–21*

"He did it first." These words are familiar to anyone who has ever worked with a group of children. They are the way the young justify inappropriate behavior—they are merely following the lead of someone else. It's a way of saying, "I'm not responsible. He did it first, and that makes it okay."

The he-did-it-first syndrome provides great direction for the action Christ encourages in today's Bible reading. Christ encourages us to love our fellow man. Then He reminds us that He did it first. How well we know the direction of God's action. God in His goodness sought us out. He took the first step. He showed us His love. "While we were yet sinners, Christ died for us." Could there be a greater display of love than this selfless, saving action?

The dimensions of Christ's love are unfathomable. He loves the whole world. He loves the hated. He loves the unlovable. He loves His tormentors. He calls us to love—He did it first.

Then He reminds us that if we cannot love the people around us whom we see, we cannot love God whom we cannot see. God urges us to practice loving those around us as a perfect way to practice loving Him.

He did it first. Our God has touched our lives through the boundless love that caused Him to send His own dear Son to the cross. He did it first. His love conquered sin, death, and the devil. He did it first. He rose victorious and took away the sting of death for those of us who follow after Him. May we follow His loving example, empowered to action by the gift of the Holy Spirit.

Prayer
Thank You, God, for first showing Your great love to me. Move me to action with the pattern of Your love. Amen.

Activity
Write a letter to a family member as a reminder of your love.

✠

Builds Up

We know that we all possess knowledge.
Knowledge puffs up, but love builds up.
1 Corinthians 8:1b

What can knowledge do for you? It can give you the edge on a business deal. It can help you with life decisions. It can elevate your position and make you feel superior to others. But this type of knowledge commands a self-seeking attitude. Today's Bible selection puts knowledge in perspective and contrasts it with love. Love is not self-seeking; love builds up. It helps others feel good about themselves and what they are doing.

In any working situation, knowledge is important. No one disavows the needs for facts. But the oil that makes relationships run smoothly is love. Love finds the good in others' ideas. Love promotes others and puts self in second place. Love smoothes over hurts and calms arguments by seeing the other perspective, and helping diffuse anger with positive words.

So where does this love come from? Perhaps you feel that your working situation could use an extra dose today. Look to the greatest love of all. Glance to the cross and see love that builds us up in the knowledge that Jesus loved us enough to give His life for us.

Model Christ's love. Seek the power of the Holy Spirit to put it in action even in difficult times. Let His indwelling give you this building-up kind of love that replaces arguing and divisiveness with unity and peace.

Whom can you build up today? What words can you share that will lift the spirits of a co-worker? Ask for God's guidance in deflating your pride when you feel puffed up and full of yourself. Build up others with the love that Christ alone can give.

Prayer

Lord, I know that knowledge is sometimes self-seeking. Infuse my knowledge with Your love, and let me use this love to build up others. Amen.

Activity

Take a scrap of wood. Write a positive message to a co-worker as a building-up block.

Mutual Edification

Let us therefore make every effort to do what leads to peace and to mutual edification. Romans 14:19

Few things in life can be done successfully without effort. The concert pianist practices daily. The gymnast progresses through constant effort and trial. A great speaker will tell you that it takes effort to plan and prepare a speech and make the presentation involving and effective.

The process of working together as members of the body of Christ is no different. It takes effort to work together in peace and harmony. Each person must be willing to let some of himself go for the good of the body of Christ. Each person must seek to do things that build up others, and that benefits the sum of the group.

Where does the energizing for such effort take place? It takes place at the foot of the cross. Here the Christian sees the perfect model of self-less giving. Even in death Jesus forgave those who persecuted Him and thought about the needs of those close to Him.

On our own we would seek to serve ourselves and not take the effort to edify others. With the power of the Holy Spirit our Gospel team can celebrate achievement, unity, and peace.

Prayer

Dear Holy Spirit, fill me with Your power so that I can make the effort to work together with colleagues and build them up. Let the world see that You live within me and my fellow workers, and give us the peace that comes from Your indwelling. Amen.

Activity

Ask God's blessing and make an effort to do something kind for someone with whom you have a troubled relationship.

✠

Like a Star

Those who are wise will shine like the bright-
ness of the heavens, and those who lead many to
righteousness, like the stars for ever and ever.
Daniel 12:3

Many people bitten with the acting bug aspire to be
stars. They take acting classes. They try out for bit
parts. They print up their resumé and have their picture portfolio ready for display. Their fondest dream is
the big break and seeing their name in lights.

God has a clear-cut formula for stardom. Those
who reflect the light of His Son—who gave up all glory
to carry our sins to the cross—will shine like stars.

Movie stars usually achieve fame with the cost of
difficulties, rejections, and disappointments. They will
point to time, patience, and the right break as the path
to achievement. The Christian "star" also endures difficulties, rejections, and disappointments. And time
and patience are needed to lead others to righteousness. God's formula for stardom includes His ever-
present power and the guidance and help of the Holy
Spirit. The Word and Sacraments are the means which
God uses to give those who desire it a "real break."

How is your trip to stardom coming? Have you
led others to know the Savior whom you love and worship? Our God sends us out to be His winning wit-

nesses to those whose lives we touch daily. We have the opportunity to speak the Word that God's Spirit can use to lead them to the knowledge that Jesus is their personal Lord and Savior. Jesus' light shines brightly in the telling of that Good News.

Movie stardom of the world is often shortlived. Today's stars will be forgotten as the next generation gains fame. But the stars in God's kingdom enjoy eternal blessings. The message of salvation they share with others brings eternal life. God's shining stars see their names written, not temporarily in lights, but eternally in the book of life.

Prayer

Lord, help me to be a shining star in leading others to You. Bless my witness so many may have their names eternally in the book of life. Amen.

Activity

Write a fan letter to someone who has been a Christian star to you.

✠

ℳ Crown

Do not be afraid of what you are about to suffer. I tell you, the devil will put some of you in prison to test you, and you will suffer persecution for ten days. Be faithful, even to the point of death, and I will give you the crown of life. Revelation 2:10

There is a moment's hush. The audience sits waiting for the announcement. The second runner-up is announced. The first runner-up is proclaimed. Then comes the moment. The crown is handed to the winner. What a triumph! What joy over this mark of achievement!

We Christians await the crown our Savior won for us in His atoning work on the cross. Life is a continual chance for us to grow and to share our faith. And always the temptations of the world try to call us away from our final victory. Doubts creep in.

But God provides a constant anchor to keep our faith secure and fixed on the Savior. In His sacraments we receive forgiveness and strength for daily living through faith in Him. We stand on God's Word to push aside the devil and cling to its message. Fellow Christians build us up and give support when trials grow.

What a joy when God calls us home! Sometimes the wait seems long. Sometimes earthly crowns tempt us to forsake our Savior for the immediate. But the Holy Spirit keeps us strong. With His help we can hold fast to the true faith and finally attain the crown of everlasting life.

Prayer

Dear Lord, each day temptations try to lure me away from You. Help me remain faithful to You until death, that I may receive the crown of everlasting life. Amen.

Activity

Review your confirmation vows or the promises made at your Baptism.

⊕

Never Die

Jesus said to her, "I am the resurrection and the life. He who believes in Me will live, even though he dies; and whoever lives and believes in me will never die." John 11:25–26a

Imagine the crowds that would rush to buy a product if an advertisement read, "Now available—a potion that offers life forever." People are constantly seeking stop-gap measures that lengthen life. They look for new drugs. Certain diets are lauded for their ability to extend healthy life. New surgical techniques are promoted and written up in scholarly medical journals. Many look for the fountain of youth.

Every Christian knows the source for eternal life. It comes in the wonderful message of Christ that is offered in today's Gospel reading. "He who believes in Me will never die." We no longer have to fear our time of death or fret over the end of our existence.

Just when does life eternal begin? It sounds like a futuristic dream. Quite the contrary. At the moment of belief, the Christian gains life eternal. Life will never end.

For the Christian, physical death is but an entry-way. What a wonderful blessing to know when life is complicated, when everything seems transient and temporary, that we can count on never dying. We can count on life eternal in the presence of our God. We can count on a life without pain and suffering, a life of unending joy. Yes, Christian, rejoice, you will live forever!

Prayer

Dear Jesus, thank You for the wonderful blessing of knowing that life will never end. Let that be my comfort and message to others who fear death and search fruitlessly for meaning to life. Let me rejoice in the sure hope of Your glorious resurrection. Amen.

Activity

Put an obituary in a prominent place where visitors or family members will see it. Use it to start a discussion about eternal life.

✥

Never Forsaken

I was young and now I am old, yet I have
never seen the righteous forsaken or their chil-
dren begging bread. Psalm 37:25

List examples of times in your life when you felt especially close to God. Perhaps it was at the birth of a
child. Maybe it was in a time of serious illness. You
might have felt it in a time of joy with your family, or
during a special service at your church. It might have
been as you vacationed and saw a breathtaking sight.
It may have been as your served your country in a far-
off land. Wherever or whenever it was, it was no doubt
a wonderful reminder of the many promises in God's
Word that tell us we are never alone.

The psalm writer of today's message reminds us
that our God is present with us. He never forsakes us.
In many jobs, when the going gets tough, the one in
charge is the first to leave. In our job the one in charge
never leaves—no matter how difficult the situation.
Our Savior is with us every step of the way as we travel
down life's road. He guides us, gives us direction, and
makes sure that the way we go is the very best for us.

The psalm writer also reminds us of the goodness
of our God. God provides for us. We can easily look at
our many material blessings and recognize the benevolent hand of a gracious God. But these are the least

147

of the blessings each child of God counts. Think of the great blessings God daily provides us as He offers forgiveness, life, and the sure hope of salvation. These blessings are so vast, that we can never fully express our thanks for them.

What great benefits we Christian workers boast! We revel daily in God's goodness and constancy.

Prayer

Lord, how I marvel at Your benefits to me! You provide me with all I need for this life and the next. You are constantly present to strengthen and support me. Make me be willing to share Your greatness with those around me. Amen.

Activity

Write a support card to someone who needs to know that God has not forsaken them.

✠

Your Inheritance

*"Then the King will say to those on his right,
'Come, you who are blessed by My Father; take
your inheritance, the kingdom prepared for you
since the creation of the world.'" Matthew 25:34*

A bumper sticker reads "I'm spending my children's inheritance." Court battles have been fought daily over the division of inheritance. Each society has certain accepted practices when it comes to passing on valued family items.

Each Christian receives a marvelous inheritance. It is not to be divided. There is no reason to fight over it. It can never be fully spent. It is given freely and lasts for all time—won for us by Jesus' perfect life and death on the cross. As children of the heavenly Father who know Jesus as their Lord and Savior, Christians possess the gift of eternal life, planned for them from the foundations of the world. Belief in Jesus' atoning sacrifice is the supreme qualifier for rights to this unending inheritance.

Knowing that treasures in heaven are waiting for us gives Christians a unique worldview. We know the treasures of this world are temporary treasures. We put the kingdom of heaven first.

It is our relationship with God's Son that keeps us in line for our inheritance. We seek to learn more about this Savior, and our love for Him increases. We look for new ways to serve the One who has done so very much to win this inheritance for us.

People who inherit earthly estates often keep the good news of the inheritance to themselves, hoping to guard against any division of the inheritance. We Christians want to share our inheritance with all. Our joy increases as the inheritance is shared, for we know Jesus came to share the gift of eternal life with all people.

Prayer
Dear Jesus, keep me ever founded in You that I may know the joy of my inheritance. Let me share the news of my inheritance with others who do not know the joy of eternal life. Amen.

Activity
Look at your will. Be sure you have included a testimony to your Christian inheritance—eternal life.

✠

My Father's House

*"Do not let your hearts be troubled. Trust in
God; trust also in Me. In My Father's house are
many rooms; if it were not so, I would have told
you. I am going there to prepare a place for you.
And if I go and prepare a place for you, I will
come back and take you to be with Me that you
also may be where I am." John 14:1–3*

The soldier in a strange land, the weary business trav-
eler, the hospital patient, and student away at college—
all share a common thought during holidays. They wish
to be home. Thoughts wander and hearts skip a beat
at thoughts of the caring and companionship which
mean "home."

In today's reading Jesus is talking to His disciples.
His time on earth is growing short. The disciples learn
that He will leave them. Oh, how they wish to go along!
But Jesus has a job for them to do. It is not yet time
for them to follow Him. He comforts them with a
promise. He is going to prepare a room in His Father's
house. He is getting things ready and one day will take
them to be with Him there. Jesus will take them home.

They know the way to His Father's house. They
have studied that way with Him. They know that Jesus
alone is the way through His atoning work on the cross.
When the world surrounds them, when they are lonely

and fearful, they can cling to the promise that one day they will go home.

We, too, hold on to that promise with firm conviction. We wait with direction. We share the route home with others who do not know the way. And when the hours are long and the going gets tough, we look toward home.

Prayer
Thank You, Lord, that I know the way home. Give me strength and spirit to share the way with others who do not yet know the path. Amen.

Activity
Put up a road map and superimpose a cross on it. When the days get difficult, remember you are headed home.

✠

Grief to Joy

Jesus saw that they wanted to ask Him about this, so He said to them, "Are you asking one another what I meant when I said, 'In a little while you will see Me no more, and then after a little while you will see Me?' I tell you the truth, you will weep and mourn while the world rejoices. You will grieve, but your grief will turn to joy. . . . Now is your time of grief, but I will see you again and you will rejoice, and no one will take away your joy." John 16:19–20, 22

The clouds well up. Darkness descends. Rain pelts down. Lightning flashes. Thunder roars. Then in an instant, the sun breaks forth and a rainbow emerges. What a change! What a contrast!

Jesus says the same is true for every Christian. In the world we are constantly pelted by storms of life. Countless forces call us to conform to the world, to cheat, to steal, to engage in sexual immorality. The world tempts us to set priorities based on material possessions, fame, power. We live in the world but not of the world. That coupled with other earthly sorrows can easily lead us to grief and despair.

The disciples knew grief only too well. They had spent years beside their Savior. Now Jesus was leaving them. But He did not leave them without support and hope. He promised that in time their grief would turn to joy. They would be together with Him again.

Thanks be to God that one day our grief will also turn to joy. Because Jesus suffered all the grief of our sins on the cross, we receive God's forgiveness and the promise of eternal life. In the twinkling of an eye, we will experience the presence of our Savior and eternal bliss.

Prayer
Dear Jesus, when life is hard and grief surrounds me, remind me of the eternal joy that awaits me in my heavenly home. Amen.

Activity
Thank God for a time when He changed a difficult time to a time of joy.

⊕

A New Order

*He will wipe every tear from their eyes.
There will be no more death or mourning or crying or pain, for the old order of things has passed
away. Revelation 21:4*

Uncertainty accompanies new orders and changes. A
new school brings concerns for the first-time student.
What will the teachers be like? Will I be able to find
my way around? Will I make new friends?

A new boss or administrator raises questions in
employees' minds. What will be expected? Will we be
able to work together? How will the organizational pattern change?

God tells us about a new order that will take place
when the world ends. It will be established by our Savior Jesus Christ. We suffer no anxiety or concern over
this new order. God makes it clear how wonderful this
new order will be. There will be no more crying or
pain. Imagine a life without sadness. Imagine perfect
bliss and constant joy.

Those of us who live daily with the indwelling
Christ see glimpses of this new order. The joy of worshiping our God with fellow Christians is often called
"a foretaste of the feast divine." We need not question
the blessedness of the "new order." We look forward
with joy to Christ's return. We know that our Savior,

Jesus Christ, won us forgiveness and new life in His redeeming work on the cross. Come, Lord Jesus.

Prayer
Dear Jesus, I wait for the new age You will establish upon Your return. I long for life in Your eternal kingdom. Amen.

Activity
Make a list of the things you look forward to in the new age at Christ's return.

✠

Come, Lord Jesus

He who testifies to these things says, "Yes, I am coming soon." Amen. Come, Lord Jesus. Revelation 22:20

There is nothing like receiving a letter from a distant family member or friend stating that soon they will be arriving for a visit. Images of past times together flash through the mind. We begin to plan sleeping quarters and favorite meals. Expectation and excitement are the bywords of the day. We write back, "Come soon. We can hardly wait! We are ready."

Jesus sends us a similar message. In His Word He tells us, "Yes, I am coming soon." Those of us in the church look across time. We count the years since Christ's departure. We question the word "soon," and then we remember the eternal nature of our God and His perspective on time.

Yes, He is coming. Each time earthquakes jostle our world, each time we hear of wars and rumors of wars, we question, "Now, Lord? Is this the time of Your return?"

Daily, the Christian assured of forgiveness and eternal life through Jesus' atoning death on the cross calls out, "Amen. Come, Lord Jesus." We eagerly await our Savior's arrival. We know what a glorious and happy age His return ushers in. We look forward to living in the presence of our God and worshiping with unending joy. We know we are ready. We live in the afterglow of the promises Jesus has given us that He has mansions prepared for us.

Many of us pray "Come, Lord Jesus" daily at meals. Let us think of the eternal dimension of this prayer: Return, Lord, and usher in a new order of time. Bring us to the glorious day when we may sit at Your right hand. "Come, Lord Jesus." We are ready.

Prayer

Come, Lord Jesus. I am ready. Help me to get the message out that will prepare others for life in Your glorious kingdom. Amen.

Activity

Use the "Come, Lord Jesus" prayer with a group this week. Help them to focus on the eternal dimension of this prayer.

⌗

Well Done

"His master replied, 'Well done, good and faithful servant! You have been faithful with a few things; I will put you in charge of many things. Come and share your master's happiness!'" Matthew 25:21

It is fun to share words of praise. In a classroom they bring out the best in many children. Words of praise encourage and show approval. Have you spoken some words of praise today? Maybe you hear yourself saying "Good job," "That's the way," "Awesome," and "I'm proud of you."

We enjoy hearing words of praise too. We're glad when someone recognizes the efforts we have made. We like to feel appreciated and successful. We especially look forward to words of praise as part of our eternal retirement package. We all want to hear our Savior saying, "Well done. You've been faithful. Share my joy eternally."

What does God expect of us? What words bring this wonderful compliment? Is it the person who brings in the most money for the kingdom? Do notches for most people saved count? No, our Lord calls us only to be faithful. He challenges us to use the talents and abilities He has given us to their fullest.

And what is our task? Our task is the privilege of sharing God's wonderful news of salvation. It is seeking and using opportunities and talents as a way to share the message of the Savior who suffered, died, and rose again. It is receiving and sharing Christ's forgiveness for times when we have failed at our job. It is letting the Holy Spirit live and motivate us to service which would be impossible without His presence.

The world may never count us as successful. Yet Jesus has already won the ultimate success for us. As we share the eternal riches Christ makes ours, we long for the day we will hear Him say, "Well done."

Prayer

Dear heavenly Father, often the world counts success by level of achievement or dollar income. Help me to see that real success comes from serving You faithfully. I look forward to hearing those wonderful words, "Well done," as I enter my heavenly home. Amen.

Activity

List words of praise. Use them as sincere compliments for people you touch today.